What the experts

101 Things Everyone Shou

"Michels and Levy have created a book that could be called 'How to Learn Science Without Really Trying'! With over one hundred questions on things we've all wondered about, the book provides answers in a succinct, cleverly written, and understandable format. An authoritative overview of science, this book fills an empty niche and should be on everyone's bookshelf!"
—Katrina L. Kelner, Ph.D., deputy editor of life sciences, *Science* magazine

"In *101 Things Everyone Should Know About Science*, children and adults alike find clear and engaging explanations of complex phenomena. Michels and Levy's book not only provides us with answers, but, more importantly, gives us the tools to ask the next question, and the next, and the next . . . *101 Things Everyone Should Know About Science* encourages a lifetime of curiosity about the world around us!"
—Julie Edmonds, Ph.D., co-director, Carnegie Academy for Science Education

"In *101 Things Everyone Should Know About Science*, Dia Michels and Nathan Levy capture the essence of science with pithy, engaging explanations. Their book challenges our understanding, intrigues us, and leads us on a voyage of discovery. This is essential reading for anyone who wants to know how things work—from lizards to light bulbs."
—April Holladay, author of *USA Today's* online science column *WonderQuest*

"Michels and Levy have created a fun science-conversation space for both adults and children! Its refreshing tone fills the very real gap between detailed texts and science trivia books. Well-researched and easy to read, this book encourages you to refresh your current science knowledge and then start asking more questions about how the world works. Get hold of *101 Things Everyone Should Know About Science* and start expanding your science knowledge today!"
—Geeta Verma, Ph.D., assistant professor of science education, Georgia State University

"*101 Things Everyone Should Know About Science* is not your ordinary book! Filled with fun facts and concise explanations, this book is sure to generate lively conversation and debate, and provide insight into essential scientific principles for people of all ages. Though targeted at children, many teenagers and adults will also benefit from the low-key refresher course this book provides. If only science textbooks were as open-ended and easy to understand as this fascinating volume is!"

—Patrick Farenga, co-author of *Teach Your Own: The John Holt Book of Homeschooling*

"Fun, accurate, and understandable, *101 Things Everyone Should Know About Science* is as engaging as it is educational. Readers will devour the book and be left eager for the 102nd thing to know! With expert text and clear illustrations, Michels and Levy appeal straight to our natural curiosity about how the physical world works."

—Margaret Kenda, Ph.D., author of *Science Wizardry for Kids*

"Science and technology play an increasingly important role in the twenty-first century. Understanding science has become critical for competing in the global workforce, making consumer decisions, taking care of older generations, educating younger generations, and leading fuller lives. *101 Things Everyone Should Know About Science* is a concise, intriguing, and valuable tool to help people learn the basics they need in this new society. I commend the authors for compiling so much essential information into this manageable format!"

—Chieh-san Cheng, president, Global Science and Technology Inc., Greenbelt, MD

"*101 Things Everyone Should Know About Science* is an impressive source of science information for all ages. I will enjoy reading it with my children and grandchildren. It's an ideal way to connect with each other and at the same time learn something of value together. It's also a great way to gain knowledge that I missed out on during my years in school!"

—Shoshana Hayman, director, Life Center, Tel Aviv, Israel

Teaching the science of everyday life

101

Things Everyone Should Know About Science

Dia L. Michels and Nathan Levy

Science, Naturally!, LLC
Washington, DC

Copyright © 2006, by Dia L. Michels and Nathan Levy
First edition • June 2006
ISBN-10: 0-9678020-5-9 / ISBN-13: 978-0-9678020-5-3

Published in the United States by
  Science, Naturally!
  627 A Street, NE
  Washington, DC 20002
  (202) 465-4798 / Toll-free: 1-866-SCI-9876 (1-866-724-9876)
  Fax: (202) 558-2132
  Info@ScienceNaturally.com / www.ScienceNaturally.com

Distributed to the book trade in the United States by
  National Book Network
  (301) 459-3366 / Toll-free: 1-800-787-6859 / Fax: (301) 429-5746
  CustServ@nbnbooks.com / www.nbnbooks.com

Cartoons by Sidney Harris, reprinted with permission from Sidney Harris
(ScienceCartoonsPlus.com).

Image of baby Einstein reading *Science* reprinted with permission from American
Association for the Advancement of Science (AAAS), Washington, DC.

Mammal illustrations reprinted with permission from *If My Mom Were A Platypus:
Mammal Babies and their Mothers*, by Dia L. Michels, illustrated by Andrew Barthelmes,
Platypus Media, 2005, ISBN: 1-930775-35-0.

Library of Congress Cataloging-in-Publication Data

Michels, Dia L.
  101 things everyone should know about science / Dia L. Michels and Nathan Levy.— 1st ed.
    p. cm. — (101 things everyone should know)
  Includes bibliographical references and index.
1. Science—Popular works. I. Title: One hundred one things everyone should know about
science. II. Title: One hundred and one things everyone should know about science. III. Levy,
Nathan. IV. Title. V. Series.
  Q162.M597 2006
  500—dc22

                                  2005023194

10 9 8 7 6 5 4 3 2 1

Schools, libraries, government and non-profit organizations may receive a bulk discount
for quantity orders. Please contact us at the address above or email us at
Info@ScienceNaturally.com.

Test booklets available (ISBN-10: 0-9678020-4-0 / ISBN-13: 978-0-9678020-4-6). See
page 159 for more details or contact us at the address above.

This book was inspired by actual events.

Advisory Committee

It takes a village to write a science education book. The authors conceived and created the book, but dozens of other people contributed copious amounts of time, energy, creativity and knowledge to make this book more interesting, more concise and more accurate.

The authors would like to thank these advisory committee members who so graciously and generously contributed to this project.

Fenton Blake, MSC, MRSC, Chemistry
Susan Buckley, B.Sc., Environmental Studies
Howard Burrows, Ph.D., Physiology and Biophysics
Rachel Connelly, Ph.D., Economics
Jean M. Rinaldi Curtacci, RN, SNM
Marisa Frieder, Ph.D., Microbiology
Martha Allen Godin, MS, Environmental Science
J. Anthony Gualtieri, Ph.D., Physics
George E. Heimpel, Ph.D., Entomology
Barbara G. Levine, MA, Math Education
Ryan McAllister, Ph.D., Physics and Biophysics
Kenneth McElwain, Ph.D., Biology
Elise McKenna, RN, Public Health and Health Education
Mark McKinnon, PA-C, Public Health
H. Michael Mogil, MS, CCM, Meteorology
Marina Moses, MS, Dr.PH, Environmental and Occupational Health
Garnet Ord, Ph.D., Physics
Richard Pisarski, Ph.D., Astrophysics
Robert Reining, MS, Agricultural Economics
Patricia Sievert, MS, Physics, Physics Education
Fred Tyner, MS, Chemistry
Richard B. Winston, Ph.D., Geology
Eric Yoder, Science Writer

Contents

Introduction

I searched long and hard to find a fun science summer camp for my 14-year-old daughter, Kaely. Though we live in a major metropolitan area, there were not many choices. In the end, we flew her 1,000 miles to attend a camp at Northern Illinois University. In contrast, her little sister attended soccer camp a few blocks from home, and her brother went to musical theater camp just down the road.

Sports camps are abundant. Drama camps are plentiful. Science camps are another story—there are far fewer of them. Because many people consider science too difficult and too tangential to normal life, it is often seen as a specialty field of study reserved for just "the really nerdy kids."

I don't think Kaely will become a professional scientist. That is precisely why it is so important for me to make sure that she and her siblings have regular exposure to science topics. She may not even take any science classes beyond her school requirements, so the necessity for additional learning is clear—not being a scientist does not excuse you from understanding science.

How disappointed I would be if my children couldn't figure out a restaurant tip, didn't appreciate the works of William Shakespeare, couldn't figure out how to find Timbuktu on a map, or had no understanding of why the United Nations was formed. By the same token, I expect them to know how hurricanes are forecast, what pasteurization means, why a circuit works, when the pH scale is useful, and what a controlled study is.

Do you know enough about science? Scientists, educators and public policy experts agree that there is a general lack of public

understanding about science. Science is one of the methods we use to attempt to understand the world around us. It helps us think about, respond to, and manipulate our world—hopefully for the better!

Understanding science can make the difference between clarity and confusion when it comes to thinking about important issues like cancer risk, space exploration, and genetically modified foods. We reap the benefits of this understanding in the technology created to generate the fuels we use to run our cars, the cleaners we use to destroy deadly microbes in our water supply, and the medical tests that may save our lives. We see the consequences of our misunderstanding in the ecological problems caused by inappropriate chemical use, the evolution of drug-resistant pathogens as a result of overuse of antibiotics, and the effect of urbanization on the earth's declining biodiversity.

Science knowledge is not as simple as memorizing a list of facts. It is, more fundamentally, the process of seeking and analyzing data in order to ask questions, producing coherent explanations or theories about how things happen, and then making rational decisions. Being able to form critical, scientific questions means that we can be involved in all kinds of active learning, from collecting and sorting to measuring, observing, analyzing, and discussing. In this age of such rapid technological advances, understanding science gives us the tools we need to keep up with and manage change.

This book asks for distinct answers to scientific questions. The challenge, though, is to redirect the focus away from looking just for the right answer, to looking for more precise and useful questions. Science is a process of curiosity. It may start with a deliberate hypothesis or it may begin with an observation from unexpected, haphazard events. But it always involves making predictions, considering all possible explanations, testing in a manner than can be duplicated, and tossing away explanations that don't fit the test results. It is a moving, growing, and constantly evolving process.

This book began as a tool for children. It expanded to become a tool for everyone—no matter what their age. It is not a trivia game or a science textbook, nor does it explain everything about science. It does not replace classroom learning, hands-on experimentation, lessons learned at home, or life experience. It can be used as a fun game for adults, a guessing game for family entertainment, a springboard for a school project, or an assessment tool for science interest and literacy.

Understanding science helps us to become more involved in the world around us. It helps us live better lives, ask better questions, and be better world citizens. Imagine a society where talking about science is as natural as talking about sports, movies, or current events. Imagine a world where people discuss science as readily over the dinner table as they discuss politics. In fact, researchers tell us that people who have an enhanced knowledge of science feel they can make a difference in management and policy decisions, which leads to increased involvement in politics and political institutions.

To care about science literacy is to care about ourselves, our communities, and our planet. Scientific literacy enables us all to make a positive difference in our world.

—*Dia*

June 2006

11

Biology Questions

Answer the questions in the following sections as best as you can, then check your answers in the corresponding answer section. The answers to the biology questions can be found starting on page 35.

1. Scientists classify organisms into groups, called kingdoms, based on fundamental similarities and common ancestry. Name some of the kingdoms.

2. "Survival of the fittest" is a theory of evolution proposed by:
      a) Albert Einstein.   c) Sir Isaac Newton.
      b) Charles Darwin.   d) Benjamin Banneker.

3. Match the animal with its class:

Monkey	Amphibian
Iguana	Bird
Pigeon	Mammal
Spider	Insect
Crab	Reptile
Frog	Crustacean
Ladybug	Arachnid

4. Name some characteristics of all mammals.

5. What is the first food for all newborn mammals?

6. What is it called when animals sleep or remain inactive during the winter?

7. What is the largest animal alive today?

8. What is the only mammal that really flies?

9. The process of an organism changing form, such as a caterpillar into a butterfly, is called _____.

10. In the carbon cycle, which of the following removes carbon dioxide from the air—plants or animals?

11. Name two ways seeds and pollen are dispersed.

12. What is the liquid called that comes from maple trees and is used to make maple syrup?

13. How many legs do all insects have?

14. Name some parasites that you or your pets could host.

15. Name three of the bodily fluids.

16. The heart pushes blood into your _____ and _____.

17. What is normal body temperature for humans?

18. If someone's body temperature falls abnormally low, he may be suffering from:

    a) hypothermia.   c) dysthermia.
    b) hyperthermia.

19. Which one of the following describes the process by which substances are heated in order to kill harmful microbes?

    a) pasteurization   c) syndication
    b) homogenization   d) hydraulics

20. Chicken pox, AIDS, and the common cold are caused by:

    a) bacteria.   c) viruses.
    b) fungi.   d) venom.

21. Scientists report that the number of species on our planet is declining dramatically. What is the primary cause of this?

22. Name four ways public health officials work to prevent disease and promote health.

Chemistry Questions

(The answers to these questions start on page 59.)

23. What are the three states of water?

24. What are the two elements that make up water?

25. Does it take longer to boil water at low altitudes or at high altitudes?

26. When you stir two cups of sugar into one cup of hot water, you end up with less than three cups of syrup. Why?

27. What mineral is found in a saline solution?

28. To make a dilute solution of salt and water more concentrated, one could:

    a) cool the solution.   c) add more water.

    b) add more salt.   d) pour some of the solution out.

29. Why do we put salt on roads and sidewalks when they are icy?

30. What is the primary mineral responsible for keeping bones strong?

31. What scale do we use to measure the acidity or alkalinity of a solution?

32. What do we use calories to measure?

33. What is the name of the chart that lists all the known elements?

34. Diamonds come from:
    a) carbon.   c) iron.
    b) water.   d) oxalates.

35. At room temperature, some elements are gas, some are liquid, but most are _____.

36. When heated, how does the volume of a gas change?

37. An atom is made up of protons, neutrons, and _____.

38. Where are most metals naturally found?
    a) in decaying trees   c) in the stratosphere
    b) in the ground   d) in flowing rivers

39. Which one of the following elements is not a metal?
    a) mercury   c) copper
    b) sodium   d) sulfur

40. Every element has an atomic mass. What does this number represent?

41. The way we express the time it takes for atoms in a radioactive substance to disintegrate is called:
      a) entropy.   c) inertia.
      b) decomposition.   d) half-life.

42. Fire needs _____ to continue burning.
      a) oil   c) paper or wood
      b) wind   d) oxygen

43. What happens over time when iron is exposed to oxygen?

44. What happens when you combine baking soda and vinegar?

45. What is the difference between a chemical change and a physical change?

Physics Questions

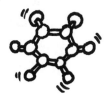

(The answers to these questions start on page 79.)

46. Sir Isaac Newton taught us that for every action (or force) there is an equal and opposite _____.

47. If an object is moving, it has energy. What do we call this energy?

48. Name a machine that operates without any external power source.

49. At the same pressure, which is more dense—hot air or cold air?

50. Who discovered the relationship between energy (E), mass (m), and the speed of light (c), as expressed in the equation $E=mc^2$?

      a) Marie Curie   c) Albert Einstein

      b) Louis Pasteur   d) Sir Isaac Newton

51. Name two of the three forces that act on objects without touching them.

52. What keeps the planets orbiting around the sun, and makes things fall to the ground?

53. What color would you see if you were to shine a red, blue, and yellow light on the same place on a white piece of paper?

54. Name some imaging techniques that allow you to see something you wouldn't be able to see with just your eyes.

55. How would you make a sonic boom?

56. Why is walking on ice or driving on wet roads so difficult?

57. We get energy to heat and cool our homes and run machines from many sources. Name as many sources of energy as you can.

58. When you flip on a light switch, the light turns on. Why?

59. How can you use a lemon to light a light bulb?

60. What is an efficient way to convert electrical current into light that generates almost no heat?

61. How does a semiconductor work?

62. Why is the sound of an approaching ambulance different from the sound of an ambulance going away from you?

63. If you were to build a bridge out of a pile of stones, the shape you would create is called _____.

64. If you had two crowns, one of pure gold and one of gold mixed with silver, how could you tell them apart without using a scale or destroying them?

65. The quickest way to cool a bottle of soda is to place it:
   a) in a bucket of ice.
   b) in a bucket of ice water.
   c) in a bucket of extremely cold water with no ice.
   d) outside on the porch when it is very cold.

66. Why does it hurt so much when you hit the water jumping into a swimming pool?

67. What was one of the things that helped Ludwig van Beethoven compose music even though he was deaf?

Earth Science Questions

(The answers to these questions start on page 99.)

68. When astronauts look at Earth from outer space, the planet looks blue. Why?

69. Each year, Earth revolves once around what?
      (a) the sun   (c) its axis
      (b) the moon   (d) the Milky Way

70. Is a lunar year longer or shorter than a solar year?

71. The sun is a:
      (a) planet.   (c) star.
      (b) meteor.   (d) reflection.

72. How many planets are in our solar system? Which one is closest to the sun?

73. What is the name of the layer of the atmosphere that protects us from the sun's harmful rays?

74. Gravitational pull from the moon causes shifts in bodies of water. What are these shifts called?

75. What are the three measurements we need to determine the exact location of a place?

76. What are the four major directions? In which direction does the needle of a compass point?

77. What is the earth's circumference?

78. Which place has no land, only ice: the North Pole or the South Pole?

79. The continental divide separates:
    a) which animals are nocturnal and which
    are diurnal.
    b) the Northern Hemisphere from the
    Southern Hemisphere.
    c) the direction water travels to the sea.
    d) where it rains from where it snows.

80. What covers the majority of the earth's surface?
    a) oceans   c) desert
    b) glaciers   d) grasslands

81. Most of the fresh water on this planet is stored in:
    (a) the Great Lakes.
    (b) the many rivers and streams on the earth.
    (c) reservoirs built by humans using dams.
    (d) polar ice caps.

82. The day with the most hours of sunlight occurs in
what month in the Northern Hemisphere? In the
Southern Hemisphere?

83. In the spring and fall, the hours of daylight and
darkness are the same on what two days?

84. Why is it colder an hour after sunrise than it is at
sunrise itself?

85. In a weather forecast, what is the difference between a *watch* and a *warning*?

86. During a thunderstorm, does lightning appear before or after you hear thunder?

87. Name three kinds of precipitation.

88. What elements must be present for a rainbow to appear?

89. What is the difference between a hurricane and a tornado?

90. What type of scale do seismologists use to measure the strength of an earthquake?

General Science Questions

(The answers to these questions start on page 121.)

91. What does the suffix "ology" mean?

92. What is a hypothesis?

93. What are the two most common measurements of temperature?

94. How many pounds does one cup of water weigh?

95. Which weighs more: a ton of apples or a ton of feathers?

96. When scientists are performing an experiment, they make changes to the conditions that brought about a particular phenomenon to see how those changes affect what they are studying. How many things do scientists change at a time?

97. Why do scientists wear white lab coats?

98. What is a control group?

99. What is the goal of a double-blind, placebo-controlled study?

100. Name some important motives for studying science.

101. In ancient Greece, what were scientists called?

Bonus Questions

(The answers to these questions start on page 131.)

Biology

What percentage of all mammals are carnivores?

Physics

How tall does a flat mirror have to be for you to see your entire image reflected in it?

Chemistry

What metal is a liquid at room temperature?

Earth Science

Throughout history, people have fought wars over natural resources such as salt, land, and oil. Scientists are concerned that another resource will be the reason for the next global conflict. What resource is it?

General Science

What is the source of all energy on Earth?

Biology
Answers

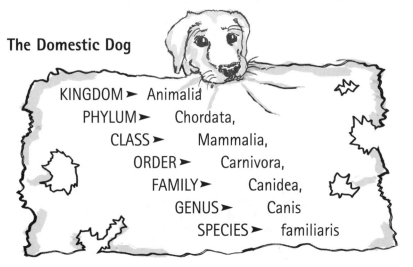

The Domestic Dog

KINGDOM ➤ Animalia
PHYLUM ➤ Chordata,
CLASS ➤ Mammalia,
ORDER ➤ Carnivora,
FAMILY ➤ Canidea,
GENUS ➤ Canis
SPECIES ➤ familiaris

1. Scientists classify organisms into groups, called kingdoms, based on fundamental similarities and common ancestry. Name some of the kingdoms.

The five kingdoms are Animalia, Plantae, Protista, Monera, and Fungi.

The classification system was begun by Carl Linnaeus in the eighteenth century. Realizing the chaos caused by the lack of a central system, he came up with the idea of one universal way of classifying organisms. His system, called binomial nomenclature, or identification by genus and species, is still used today.

The classification system (also known as taxonomy) begins with the kingdom designation. The next label is phylum, which is called the division when referring to plants. Phyla are divided into classes, which are further broken down into orders. Each order is divided into families, which are broken into genera, and each genus is divided into species. The system allows organisms to be grouped, with increasing precision, by their attributes. For example, all animals with backbones are in the kingdom Animalia and the phylum Chordata. (An easy way to remember "kingdom, phylum, class, order, family, genus, species" is to use the sentence "King Phillip Came Over For Good Sausage.") You can even go further and be more specific, using a suborder and superfamily.

A good example of an animal classification is the domestic dog, which is in the Animalia kingdom, phylum Chordata, class Mammalia, order Carnivora, family Canidae, genus *Canis*, species *familiaris*. In English this means animal with a nerve cord (and a spine), breasts for feeding its young, teeth for eating meat, dog-like, and domesticated. The dandelion classification is: Plantae, Magnoliophyta, Magnoliopsida, Asterales, Asteraceae, *Taraxacum, officinale*.

Scientific names are often referred to with the two-word names of the genus and species, such as *Canis familiaris* for a dog or *Homo sapiens* for a human. Using scientific names allows people who speak different languages to communicate and helps avoid confusion with common names for species. Each scientific name is unique and refers to only one species, which is important because so many new species are being discovered. When Linnaeus created this system, he expected only fifteen thousand species ever to be named. Today there are between 1.5 and 2 million named organisms—with more coming every day.

2. "Survival of the fittest" is a theory of evolution proposed by:
      a) Albert Einstein   c) Sir Isaac Newton
☞ **b) Charles Darwin   d) Benjamin Banneker**

Charles Darwin developed the theory of evolution in the mid-nineteenth century. His principle of natural selection, or "survival of the fittest," was based on many observations of differences between members of the same species, especially a group of finches. Darwin theorized that random variations led to a situation in which some individuals of the same species adapted better to their environment, and were therefore more likely to survive and produce offspring with that same variation. Darwin noted differences among thirteen species of finches that were isolated from each other: they all had different beaks and their behavior varied. Darwin proposed that these finches all evolved from one common species. Modern DNA analysis has proven this to be true.

Sir Isaac Newton was an English physicist, mathematician, and astronomer who is famous for his three laws of motion. (See questions 46 and 50.)

Albert Einstein, recognized as one of the greatest physicists of all time, proposed the theory of relativity. (See question 100.)

Benjamin Banneker was a free black man during the time of slavery who owned a farm near Baltimore, Maryland, and helped lay out the design of the city of Washington, DC. He also made the first American clock.

3. Match the animal with its class:

Monkey	Amphibian
Iguana	Bird
Pigeon	Mammal
Spider	Insect
Crab	Reptile
Frog	Crustacean
Ladybug	Arachnid

Monkeys are mammals—warm-blooded animals covered in hair. There are about about 4,200 known species of mammals alive today, including humans, giraffes, rats, and dolphins. (See questions 4, 5, and 8.)

Iguanas are reptiles—cold-blooded, scaly-skinned animals with backbones. Reptiles usually lay eggs and have claws on their toes. Because they are cold-blooded, they need to use their environment to adjust their body temperature. There are about 6,000 living species of reptiles, including snakes, lizards, turtles, and alligators.

Pigeons are birds—endothermic (or warm-blooded), back-boned animals that lay eggs, have skin covered with feathers, and have wings. There are about 9,000 species of birds alive, including hummingbirds, flamingos, pigeons, and penguins.

Spiders are arachnids—animals with eight walking legs, a body divided into two parts (the cephalothorax and the abdomen), and no antennae. Spiders are in the same phylum as insects and crustaceans. There are approximately 35,000 species of spiders, including moss spiders, jumping spiders, camel spiders, and tarantulas.

Crabs are crustaceans—animals with two pairs of antennae and an exoskeleton that needs to be shed as the animal grows. They are mostly found in water environments and they lay eggs. Crustaceans are invertebrates, which means they don't have a backbone. They breathe through gills and are cold-blooded. There are about 44,000 species of crustaceans, including lobsters, shrimp, and crayfish.

Frogs are amphibians—cold-blooded vertebrate animals. They lay eggs and have smooth skin without scales, hair, or feathers. Because of their skin, they need a moist environment to survive. There are about 5,700 species of amphibians, including toads, salamanders, and caecilians (which look like snakes and live underground).

Ladybugs are insects—cold-blooded invertebrates with hard exoskeletons, jointed legs, and segmented bodies that consist of a head, thorax, and abdomen. The head has one pair of antennae, one pair of compound eyes, three pairs of simple eyes, and three pairs of mouth parts. Scientists estimate that there are well over one million species of insects, including flies, bees, mosquitoes, and cockroaches. (See question 13.)

4. Name some characteristics of all mammals.

All mammals have backbones, are warm-blooded, have hair or fur, and drink their mother's milk when they are born.

All mammals are vertebrates, which means they have backbones, unlike worms or insects. They are also able to maintain a constant body temperature, which is called being warm-blooded. Mammals have hair or fur at some point in their lives, and the females produce milk for their young through mammary glands. (See question 5.) Mammals have large brains with modified skulls, complex teeth, and three ear bones. Their skulls have adapted over time to support their elaborate chewing muscles, and to better contain their large brains. Scientists believe that mammalian ear bones (the malleus, incus, and stapes) evolved from bones that were no longer needed, such as a bone to support gills. There are three orders of mammals: monotremes (egg-layers), marsupials (pouched mammals), and placentals (which accounts for the majority of mammals, including humans).

5. What is the first food for all newborn mammals?

Mother's milk.

All female mammals possess glandular tissue that can secrete milk. A complete food, it contains everything a newborn mammal needs. Different mammals have different needs, and so naturally they produce different milk. The milk produced by a female deer is different from the milk produced by a female whale or a female human. Each mammal produces milk with the perfect combination of fat, protein, carbohydrates, vitamins, and minerals to enable their species to thrive. Breastmilk is a living biological fluid. It contains hormones, growth factors, immunoglobulins (proteins that help fight disease), and anti-inflammatory components that stimulate and support the growth of the nursing baby's immune system and organ development. (See question 4.)

Before artificial mammal milk was created in the nineteenth century, any mammal young for whom breastmilk was unavailable faced almost certain death. Today, artificial milk can save lives, but it pales in comparison to the milk made naturally.

Humans are the only species that consume milk beyond childhood, and the only species who ingest the milk of any other mammal. Around the globe, humans consume milk products from cows, goats, sheep, and even water ox, in the form of milk, cheese, butter, yogurt, and ice cream.

6. What is it called when animals sleep or remain inactive during the winter?

Hibernation.

Hibernation is the period of reduced activity experienced in the winter by many animals. Small animals with high metabolic rates, such as rodents, hummingbirds, bats, etc., are true hibernators. When food is hard to find and the weather is cold, a hibernating animal will hide in a safe place and lower its metabolic rate (how fast it burns energy) by reducing its heart rate. This brings the animal's body temperature down— below the outside temperature. It then lives from stored energy, like fat. If its body temperature drops too low, the hibernator may burn more energy for a while to bring its body temperature back up to a safe level. It might also "wake" to eat when its energy stores are low. Some hibernating animals, such as chipmunks, store food in an underground maze of tunnels and storerooms for when they wake to eat.

Other animals, such as bears, experience something very close to hibernation, spending much of the winter in a deep sleep and fasting (not eating). The hibernating bear's temperature and metabolic rate only drops a little, however, and it may even wake on warmer days to eat and move about.

7. What is the largest animal alive today?

The blue whale.

The largest animal that has ever lived is the blue whale, whose scientific name is *Balaenoptera musculus*. It can reach a size of one hundred feet long (30.48 m) and weigh up to three hundred thousand pounds (136,000 kg)—as much as 1,600 people or thirty-two elephants. It is larger than the *Tyrannosaurus rex* and *Apatosaurus* combined. The African elephant, the world's largest land animal alive today, could fit on a blue whale's tongue.

Whales are mammals. They produce milk for their young and are warm-blooded. Blue whales are found throughout the earth's oceans, and they migrate great distances—between polar waters (where they live) and warmer waters (where they give birth). Their diet consists of tiny shrimp-like animals called krill. During the summer feeding season, a blue whale can eat as many as forty million krill a day. Sadly, due to twentieth-century whaling, blue whales are now endangered, with only an estimated eleven thousand left in the world.

8. What is the only mammal that really flies?

The bat.

Bats, just like humans, are mammals. They have fur and are warm-blooded vertebrates that produce milk through mammary glands to feed their young. Bats are the only actual flying mammals. (The deceptively named "flying squirrel" does not actually have wings, only large flaps of skin it can use to glide through the air on long jumps.)

A bat's wing contains the same bones as the human arm and hand. There are about 4,200 species of mammals, and some 1,000 of them are bats, displaying an astonishing amount of diversity. The Kitti's hog-nosed bat is the size of a large bumblebee and is the smallest-known mammal in the world. The three species of vampire bats, found in South America, are the only mammals that feed on blood. The gigantic flying fox bat has a wingspan of five to six feet, making it the largest of the bats. Most bats eat insects, but some eat fruit, which plays an important role in distributing the seeds of plants.

9. The process of an organism changing form, such as a caterpillar into a butterfly, is called _____.

Metamorphosis.

Metamorphosis is the process by which some animals change form during their lives, getting closer and closer to complete adulthood. The most well-known metamorphic animal is the butterfly, which transitions from egg to caterpillar (the larva) to chrysalis (the pupa) to butterfly (the adult). Many other animals, such as insects, frogs, crustaceans, and some fishes also undergo metamorphosis.

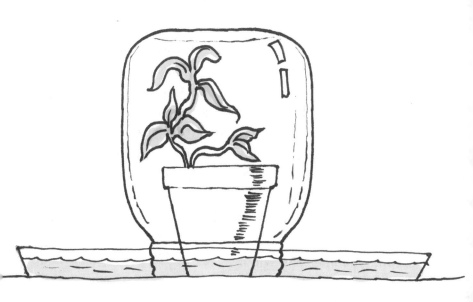

10. In the carbon cycle, which of the following removes carbon dioxide from the air—plants or animals?

Plants.

Trees and other plants produce oxygen as the first step of photosynthesis, using carbon dioxide (from the air) and water (from the ground or bodies of water) to fuel the reaction. The sugar produced by photosynthesis is converted by cellular respiration into ATP (adenosine triphosphate), the "fuel" used by all living things. Most of the time the photosynthetic process uses water and releases oxygen, which animals absolutely must have to stay alive.

In 1780, the famous English chemist Joseph Priestley found that plants could "restore air which has been injured by the burning of candles." He placed a mint plant in an upturned glass jar inside a container of water for several days. He found that "the air would neither extinguish a candle, nor was it [at] all inconvenient to a mouse [that] I put into it." In other words, he discovered that plants produce oxygen. The chemical equation that describes the process involves the reaction between carbon dioxide and water catalyzed by sunlight, which produces glucose and a so-called waste product, oxygen. The glucose sugar is either directly used as energy or stored. The waste, oxygen, is excreted into the atmosphere, where plants and animals use it for respiration. Thus, plants provide two things humans and animals need—glucose and oxygen.

11. Name two of the ways seeds and pollen are dispersed.

Water, animals, and wind.

The seeds of plants are dispersed, or spread, in many different ways. Some can float in wind or water for many days to reach far-away places. Some are eaten by animals and are then deposited elsewhere in the animals' droppings. Some are transported to new areas by humans, as well. All these transport mechanisms help a plant, as a species, to survive by expanding the area in which it lives and by reducing competition for light and nutrients between plants of the same species.

Some plants have seed pods, which burst when they become ripe. When this happens, the seeds are carried by the wind to other locations. In certain kinds of fleshy fruit, the seeds are dispersed by birds that eat those fruits and then leave droppings in another location.

Pollination is the transfer of pollen to other plants. The most common agents of pollination are flying insects (who take care of most flowering plants) and the wind (which pollinates many trees and all grasses and conifers). But crawling and hopping insects, snails, bats, primates, rodents, and hummingbirds may also serve as pollinators.

12. What is the liquid called that comes from maple trees and is used to make maple syrup?

Sap.

Sap is the liquid that moves around in plants. It travels up to the leaves, where sugar (that is produced by photosynthesis) is added. Sap then travels back through the plant, serving as food. Maple trees, like many plants, have special tissue called phloem that carries the sap throughout the tree, similar to the way our circulatory tissues carry our blood. Sap from trees has many different uses. Sap from aloe plants is used in medicines. Some saps are used as sweeteners, some are used as waterproofing compounds, and some are used as turpentine. The sap from the coconut palm, known as toddy, is even a popular drink in tropical countries!

Another example of a product made from sap is pure maple syrup, which is produced by concentrating the slightly sweet sap of the sugar maple tree. In the early spring, the sugar farmer will begin tapping his trees. If buckets are used to collect the sap, a metal spout, or spile, is tapped snugly into the hole, and a bucket is hung from a hook on the spout. A cover is put on the bucket to keep out snow, debris, insects, and scavengers. The maple tree must be a least ten inches (25.4 cm) in diameter and in good health before it can be tapped. It takes about forty gallons (151 l) of this slightly sweet sap, boiled down, to make one gallon (3.8 l) of pure maple syrup. The syrup can then be boiled down even further to make maple sugar, which can be used to make delicious candy.

13. How many legs do all insects have?

Six.

Insects have six jointed legs, as well as segmented bodies with a hard outer covering, or exoskeleton, and no backbone. Insects can be found around the world, even north of the Arctic Circle and in Antarctica. There are more than nine hundred thousand species of insects, far more than all the other animal species combined. Fossils show that insects existed 400 million years ago. Some prehistoric insects were enormous, with wing spans of twenty-seven inches (70 cm). These days, beetles are the largest of all insects. The heaviest insect on record was a pregnant giant weta beetle, a rare and endangered New Zealand species, that weighed just over two ounces (71 g). (See question 3.)

Butterflies and moths are also insects. They have wings covered with tiny, overlapping scales. In the case of butterflies, these wings are often brightly colored to discourage predators. The top speed for a butterfly is twelve miles (19.6 km) per hour, or about as fast as most people can ride a bike.

14. Name some parasites that you or your pets could host.

Fleas, mosquitoes, ticks, leeches, mites, lice, tapeworms, and heartworms.

A parasite is an organism (plant or animal) that feeds from another organism, called a host. Some common examples include fleas, mosquitoes, ticks, leeches, mites, lice, tapeworms, and heartworms. A parasite does not always harm its host, but it never does the host any good. Almost all living creatures act as a host at some time.

Parasites exist throughout nature, and live by taking nutrients from the host's body. Some parasites, such as ticks, fleas, and leeches feed on the blood of the host externally. Other parasites live inside their hosts, feeding on digested food. Parasites live all around us. They affect a wide variety of organisms; for example, aphids infest rose bushes, horse flies eat blood by biting animals, and liver flukes feed on bile in the host's liver.

15. Name three of the bodily fluids.

Blood, sweat, saliva (or spit), tears, breastmilk, semen, urine, mucus, lymph, plasma, serum, and digestive juices.

The human body is composed mostly of water, which our body uses to produce different fluids. These fluids help the body to work properly. Glands are organs in the body that create and release chemical substances through ducts. Glands produce sweat, saliva, tears, and breastmilk. Blood is comprised of two fluids and it also carries hormones, nutrients, infection-fighting cells, and oxygen. Plasma is the liquid component in the blood, while serum is the protein-rich fluid that remains after blood clots. Lymph is a milky fluid that contains lymphocytes, a type of white blood cell. It plays a critical role in the body's immune system by filtering out and destroying toxins and germs. In mature males, the reproductive system produces semen, which contains the sperm needed to reproduce. Our kidneys process urine to carry wastes out of the body. Mucus is a thick secretion made by special tissues, including the inside of the nose and throat.

The Human Heart

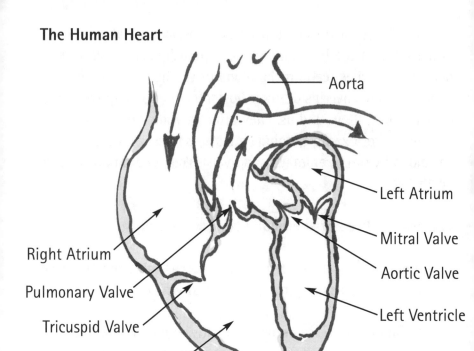

Aorta

Left Atrium

Mitral Valve

Aortic Valve

Left Ventricle

Right Atrium

Pulmonary Valve

Tricuspid Valve

Right Ventricle

16. The heart pushes blood into your _____ and _____.

Veins and arteries.

The heart, a muscular organ, pushes blood into the veins and arteries. These elements make up the circulatory system. The heart must function continuously from before a person is born until death. In an average lifetime, the human heart beats more than 2.5 billion times, without ever pausing to rest. Blood, coursing from the heart through vessels, delivers essential elements and removes harmful wastes. A series of valves within the veins prevents blood from moving backwards, and gravity is used to push blood onward, preventing it from stagnating when the push given it by the heart wears off. Without blood, the human body would stop working.

The human heart is divided into two cavities. The left cavity pumps blood through the entire body, while the right cavity pumps blood only through the lungs. The cavities are separated into two chambers. The upper chambers are called atria and the lower ones, ventricles. Oxygenated blood is carried from the heart through muscular tubes called arteries. These arteries carry blood, which is red with oxygen, to the tissues and organs of the body. Oxygen is then released into the tissues, and carbon dioxide is picked up. Veins carry this deoxygenated blood (which appears blue) back to the heart. The auricle, or atrium, is the chamber that receives blood from the body being returned to the heart by the veins. Once oxygenated by the lungs, the blood flows again through the body, starting the cycle over again.

17. What is normal body temperature for humans?

It is 98.6°F, or 37°C.

In human beings, the body temperature is 98.6°F (about 37°C), although temperatures from 97.5°F-99°F (36.4°C-37.2°C) are considered normal. Humans, like other mammals and birds, are endotherms, or warm-blooded animals. Their body temperatures remain constant through processes that heat and cool the body, such as the use of more food or fat stores for heat energy, and actions such as sweating and panting to cool down. Exotherms, or cold-blooded animals, use mainly the environment, such as the sun and shade, to raise or lower their body temperatures.

18. If someone's body temperature falls abnormally low, he may be suffering from:

 a) hypothermia   c) dysthermia
   b) hyperthermia

Hypothermia occurs when the human body's core temperature is less than its normal level; severe hypothermia sets in at 92°F (33.3°C). Between 86°F-98.6°F (30°C-37°C), a person will experience waves of violent shivering, dilated pupils, and muscular rigidity. At 86°F (30°C), the person is in a state called "metabolic icebox," where he appears icy and dead but is actually alive. The body loses heat in water about thirty times faster than in air, which is why boating accidents can be so dangerous in cold weather. If such an accident occurs, it is important to get out of the water (on top of an overturned boat or wreckage), instead of hanging onto the boat while submerged in the water. Because the body loses heat in water so quickly, it is important to get out of the water as soon as possible.

Hyperthermia describes what happens when the body's temperature rises above 98.6°F (37°C). The two most common kinds of hyperthermia are heat exhaustion and heat stroke.

Dysthermia is a disorder with symptoms such as body tremors, much like those suffered by people with epilepsy.

19. Which one of the following describes the process by which substances are heated in order to kill harmful microbes?

a) pasteurization   c) syndication
b) homogenization   d) hydraulics

Pasteurization is the process of sterilizing liquids such as milk, fruit juice, honey, eggs, wine, and even cheese, in order to destroy harmful organisms such as yeasts, molds, bacteria, and disease-causing microbes. Louis Pasteur theorized that the spoiling of perishable products could be prevented by destroying the microbes already present in these products and by protecting the sterilized material against further contamination. During the 1860s Pasteur applied this theory to the preservation of beverages and foodstuffs, introducing the technique of heat treatment now known as pasteurization. When milk is pasteurized, it is heated to 160°F (71°C) for fifteen seconds or to 145°F (63°C) for thirty minutes, and then quickly cooled to below 50°F (10°C).

Homogenization is the process of making a mixture uniform. In homogenization, hot milk, under high pressure, is forced through small nozzles. This makes the fat globules small enough (about one micrometer) to remain evenly dispersed throughout the milk.

Syndication refers to the process in journalism and entertainment by which a company purchases news, television shows, comic strips, or other features and makes them available to numerous outlets at the same time.

Hydraulics is the use of liquid to create pressure. It allows pressure to be transferred over long distances and in many directions, and has many applications. The brakes on your car, for example, use hydraulics to take the pressure you apply to the brake pedal and move it to the entire braking system.

20. Chicken pox, AIDS, and the common cold are caused by:
>   a) bacteria   c) viruses 👉
>   b) fungi   d) venom

Viruses are much smaller than bacteria, and they infect almost all life forms, including plants, animals, and even bacteria. They are made of genetic material (DNA or RNA) surrounded by a protein coat. DNA is deoxyribonucleic acid, a nucleic acid that contains the genetic instructions specifying the biological development of all cellular forms of life (and most viruses). RNA (ribonucleic acid) is like DNA except that it is almost always a single-stranded molecule with shorter chemical compound chains.

Viruses invade and infect living cells, often damaging or killing them. They can also cause disease. Some viral diseases include chicken pox (caused by the varicella-zoster virus), AIDS (caused by HIV, the human immunodeficiency virus), and the common cold. Viruses require a host. The host provides them with all the chemicals and molecules they need to survive and reproduce.

There are no cures for viral diseases. Our most effective treatments work to eliminate symptoms. Prevention of infection through the use of vaccines is currently the best medical option.

Bacteria are one-celled organisms that exist in virtually every environment on Earth, including the human body. Some are beneficial and do things such as aid in digestion. Others are harmful and can cause sickness or disease.

Fungi are organisms that obtain energy from an outside source such as soil, rotting material, or living plants. Some fungi are beneficial and can be used as food or to produce medicines and antibiotics (such as penicillin); other fungi can be poisonous.

Venoms are poisons that come from animals and are used to damage an enemy or to catch prey through a sting or bite.

21. Scientists report that the number of species on our planet is declining dramatically. What is the primary cause of this?

Habitat destruction.

The primary factor endangering many species of plants and animals on Earth is the destruction of their homes, or habitats, by humans. The number of people living on Earth has grown dramatically. In 1800, there were 980 million (.98 billion) people on the planet. By 1900, this number had risen to 1.675

billion. Today it is almost 6.5 billion. As the population rises, our need for resources such as living space, food, and fuel grows, and people have begun to move into areas that were previously unsettled.

One of the areas in which this is most prevalent is the rainforest. The rainforests are home to the largest number of species on the planet, and are being destroyed at an alarming rate in order to free up land for housing, farming, and commercial development. The destruction of even one species can have a drastic impact on many other species connected to it. For example, what would happen if one species of frog in the rainforest was wiped out? All the animals who ate that frog would suffer, because a vital part of their food supply would be gone.

Other ways that humans threaten habitats and their inhabitants include pollution, hunting, the collection and trading of plant and animal parts, and the introduction of non-native species that lack predators or control species.

22. Name four ways public health officials work to prevent disease and promote health.

Public health officials work to ensure that people receive quality health care and live in a safe and healthy environment. They conduct research and apply their findings to disease-control efforts. They build partnerships with clinics, hospitals, other health care facilities, doctors, and pharmaceutical companies to maximize access to affordable, high-quality health care. Public health professionals work in education, prevention, record keeping, and disease control.

Some public health efforts that have been instrumental in preventing disease and promoting health include:

Nutrition
• Arranging for vitamin D to be added to milk, to prevent rickets
• Arranging for folic acid to be added to flour products, to prevent spina bifida
• Arranging for iodine to be added to table salt, to prevent gout

Disease prevention
• Enforcing clean water regulations
• Establishing vaccination requirements
• Working to eliminate rats, cockroaches, etc., from food-service and urban areas
• Conducting epidemiological studies of diseases in order to prevent them (see below for specific examples)

Education
• Campaigns against smoking, consuming uncooked meat and eggs, and unnecessary use of antibiotics
• Campaigns promoting breastfeeding, seat belts, gun safety, motorcycle helmets, child vehicle restraints, and hand-washing

Epidemiology
• Investigating disease outbreaks
• Predicting emerging diseases
• Implementing preventive measures

Chemistry
Answers

23. What are the three states of water?

Liquid, solid, and gas.

Water exists in three states. We use the liquid state most often in our daily activities, for drinking, washing things, and cooking. Liquids do not hold a shape, but they maintain the same volume. In humans, liquid water makes up about 70 percent of our bodies. Ice, snow, and frost are frozen water. Water's freezing temperature—the highest temperature at which water will become solid—is 32°F (0°C).

Water vapor is water in its gaseous state. Until it reappears as a liquid or solid, it is invisible. Water evaporates into the air from bodies of water and from plant and human respiration. Water vapor is an important regulator of the earth's heat. Without it, and other so-called greenhouse gases, our planet would be very hot by day and very cold at night. A gas doesn't hold its shape or maintain its volume. For example, if you pour one liter of water from a watering can into a bucket, it's still one liter. If you take one liter of water vapor and release it into a two-liter bottle, it will spread out to fill the entire two liter bottle. At sea level, water vaporizes at 212°F (100°C).

24. What are the two elements that make up water?

Hydrogen and oxygen.

A water molecule is made up of two hydrogen atoms and one oxygen atom. Its chemical formula is H_2O. Water in its liquid and solid states—including oceans, lakes, streams, and glaciers—covers 71 percent of the world's surface, making

Earth unique among the planets. It is this abundance of water that makes life on Earth possible. But there is a delicate balance to be maintained. If there is too much water, flooding occurs, and with too little, drought will make it difficult or impossible for many plants to survive.

Water makes up 50 to 90 percent of the weight of living organisms (from bacteria to human beings), and is essential for many of the processes that occur with these organisms' cells. As humans, for example, we can go without food for several weeks, but we will die without water in only a few days. (See question 81 and the earth science bonus question.)

25. Does it take longer to boil water at low altitudes or at high altitudes?

Low altitudes.

At higher elevations (such as in Denver, Colorado—the Mile High City), the boiling point of water decreases, so it boils faster. This is because as you increase elevation, atmospheric pressure decreases (there is less atmopshere above you). To boil, the vapor pressure of a liquid must equal the vapor pressure of the air around it (the atmospheric pressure). Since atmospheric pressure is lower at higher elevations, water being heated reaches atmospheric pressure quicker (and at a lower temperature) and boils faster than it would at lower elevations. This means some foods will actually require longer cooking times at higher elevations. Check food labeling to see if there are special instructions for higher altitude cooking.

26. When you stir two cups of sugar into one cup of hot water, you end up with less than three cups of syrup. Why?

The sugar dissolves.

When sugar (sucrose—$C_{12}H_{22}O_{11}$—twelve atoms of carbon, twenty-two atoms of hydrogen, and eleven atoms of oxygen) is poured into hot water, a solution is created. Sugar, the solute, dissolves into the water, the solvent. There are no chemical changes, and the sugar and water still exist separately, but, water breaks the sugar (which is a molecular solid) into individual sugar molecules. These molecules then interact with the water and can fit "between" the water molecules without changing the water's volume. Once the water becomes saturated with sugar molecules, the addition of more sugar will result in sugar being deposited at the bottom of the container. Hence the overall volume would then increase.

27. What mineral is found in a saline solution?

Salt.

Minerals (like salt) are natural compounds formed through geological processes. Saline is the term used to describe something, including a solution, that contains salt. The chemical name for salt is sodium chloride. Oceans are huge saline solutions, containing about 3.5 percent salt. Salt is also found in some rivers, lakes, and seas (e.g., the Dead Sea and Great Salt Lake). There are natural salt beds that are thought to have come from the salt water of evaporated ancient seas. Salt manufacturers obtain salt either from these beds or by evaporating seawater. People have used salt as a seasoning and to preserve food supplies since ancient times. It was even used as money, in the form of salt cakes, by the Hebrews and other societies during Biblical times. There are references in the Christian Bible to salt and its value (e.g., "any man worth his salt"). In Roman times, salt was an important item of trade and was used as money as well. Roman soldiers received part of their pay in salt, and newborn babies were rubbed with salt to promote good health. To compare a person to the "salt of the earth" is to say that they are valuable and have worth. Before refrigeration, rubbing salt into meat was the only way to preserve it. Salt is an excellent cleaning agent, drives away ants, is an effective antiseptic, and is used in skin treatments.

Solutions of salts in water are called electrolytes. Both electrolytes and molten salts conduct electricity. Electrolytes also help the kidneys retain proper fluid levels and help balance the amounts of acids and bases in our bodies. They also help the cells in our bodies maintain a proper "voltage" so that the nerve cells can communicate with each other via electrical signals. Electrolyte drinks containing sodium and potassium salts are used to replenish the body's water and electrolyte levels after water loss. Excessive water loss, resulting in dehydration, can be caused by exercise, diarrhea, vomiting, starvation, or surgery.

28. To make a dilute solution of salt and water more concentrated, one could:
    a) cool the solution. **c) add more water.**
    b) add more salt.   **d) pour some of the solution out.**

In order to make salt water more concentrated, one must add more salt. Cooling has no effect on concentration of salt in the solution, and adding more water dilutes the solution, making it less salty. Pouring some of the solution out doesn't change the concentration, it only lessens the volume.

Another way to increase this concentration would be to let some of the solution evaporate. This could be done by slowly heating the solution, then letting it cool. Heating would speed evaporation, leaving less water and the same amount of salt. However, the quickest way to increase the concentration is to add more salt.

29. Why do we put salt on roads and sidewalks when they are icy?

Salt lowers the freezing temperature of water.

When salt is spread on icy roads, it lowers the temperature at which water turns to ice. Salt placed on the roads dissolves into the liquid water that is mixed in with the solid ice and lowers its freezing temperature, melting the ice around it. The water will not refreeze unless the air around it gets much colder. (See question 27.)

Preventive salting (salting before a snow or ice storm actually hits) and salting during and after a storm can help keep the roads safer for winter travelers. However, salt causes metal corrosion, rusting, and damage to vehicles and other metal objects. It can also wash off the roadways and get into the soil and onto plants, as well as cause dogs' paws to burn. Some alternatives to salt have been suggested, but many are more expensive or less effective. Sand is often used in place of salt. Although it does not melt ice the same way salt does—it is darker than the salt and absorbs sunlight—it also provides traction.

30. What is the primary mineral responsible for keeping bones strong?

Calcium.

Calcium is the primary mineral used by the body to keep teeth and bones strong and healthy. It doesn't do it alone though; other nutrients such as vitamin D and phosphorus are also part of the process. In fact, the body requires a certain amount of vitamin D to absorb calcium properly.

When there is not enough calcium in the bloodstream for bodily needs, including muscle contraction and blood clotting, the body will begin breaking down the bones to obtain calcium. This is one reason that calcium is so important in our diet. Some good sources of calcium are dairy products such as milk, cheese, and yogurt, as well as leafy vegetables, fish, and calcium-fortified foods such as orange juice.

31. What scale do we use to measure the acidity or alkalinity of a solution?

The pH scale.

The abbreviation pH stands for potential hydrogen. We use the pH scale to measure the alkalinity or acidity of solutions—how basic or acidic they are. Acids have a sour taste (although you should never taste strong or concentrated acids). Bases have a bitter taste (again: do not taste them) and a slippery feeling between the fingers. Both acids and bases conduct electrolytes.

The pH scale measures the concentration of positively charged hydrogen ions in a solution, assigning them values from 0 to 14. Values below 7 are considered acidic, and values above 7 are considered alkaline (basic). Pure water has a pH value of 7.0 and is considered neither acidic nor basic. Tap water coming from your kitchen faucet may have values between 6.5 and 7.5 depending upon the minerals dissolved in it. The acid in your stomach has a pH of about 2.0 (very acidic), while household ammonia has a pH of about 11.9 (basic).

32. What do we use calories to measure?

Energy.

We use calories to measure heat or energy. Scientists define the small calorie, or gram calorie (c), as the amount of heat it takes to raise the temperature of one mililiter of water 1°C. The large calorie, or kilocalorie (C), is equal to one thousand small calories and is used to measure the amount of energy produced by the food we eat. Some items we consume have no calories, like water, coffee, or artificially-sweetened drinks, and provide us with no energy—although coffee and some diet sodas contain caffeine, which can create the illusion of energy. Other foods, such as cake and doughnuts, have lots of calories, but they provide little more than energy since they are very low in nutrients. These are known as empty calories. Any extra calories we consume beyond what is needed for our daily activities are stored by the body as fat.

Periodic Table of the Elements

IA	IIA	IIIB	IVB	VB	VIB	VIIB	VII			IB	IIB	IIIA	IVA	VA	VIA	VIIA	O
1 H																	2 He
3 Li	4 Be											5 B	6 C	7 N	8 O	9 F	10 Ne
11 Na	12 Mg											13 Al	14 Si	15 P	16 S	17 Cl	18 Ar
19 K	20 Ca	21 Sc	22 Ti	23 V	24 Cr	25 Mn	26 Fe	27 Co	28 Ni	29 Cu	30 Zn	31 Ga	32 Ge	33 As	34 Se	35 Br	36 Kr
37 Rb	38 Sr	39 Y	40 Zr	41 Nb	42 Mo	43 Tc	44 Ru	45 Rh	46 Pd	47 Ag	48 Cd	49 In	50 Sn	51 Sb	52 Te	53 I	54 Xe
55 Cs	56 Ba	57 *La	72 Hf	73 Ta	74 W	75 Re	76 Os	77 Ir	78 Pt	79 Au	80 Hg	81 Tl	82 Pb	83 Bi	84 Po	85 At	86 Rn
87 Fr	88 Ra	89 +Ac	104 Rf	105 Ha	106 Sg	107 Ns	108 Hs	109 Mt	110 110	111 111	112 112	113 113					

* Lanthanide Series	58 Ce	59 Pr	60 Nd	61 Pm	62 Sm	63 Eu	64 Gd	65 Tb	66 Dy	67 Ho	68 Er	69 Tm	70 Yb	71 Lu
+ Actinide Series	90 Th	91 Pa	92 U	93 Np	94 Pu	95 Am	96 Cm	97 Bk	98 Cf	99 Es	100 Fm	101 Md	102 No	103 Lr

33. What is the name of the chart that lists all the known elements?

The periodic table.

Elements are basic chemical substances that cannot be further broken down by chemical reactions. All other compounds and substances are made of elements. The periodic table is the grouping of elements by their properties, ordering them in rows according to their atomic number, or the number of protons in their nuclei. It helps us keep track of elements by their properties. The elements are also grouped by other properties, such as whether they are noble gases or metals. Gold and silver are both considered transition metals and are grouped with other elements such as cobalt and nickel. The first periodic table was put together by Dmitri Ivanovich Mendeleev in 1864, but it grows and changes over time because scientists are constantly trying to discover new elements. (See questions 37 and 40.)

34. Diamonds come from:

 a) carbon. **c) iron.**

b) water. **d) oxalates.**

Diamonds are a form of carbon valued for their beauty in jewelry and for their hardness in industrial use. They are transparent crystals of super-bonded carbon atoms. Most diamonds are mined from volcanic pipes (part of a deep volcano structure). Here, intense pressure and heat is suitable for diamond formation. Diamonds may be ejected from their formation region within lava flows and other volcanic activity.

Diamonds are famous for being the hardest known natural substance because they are made of sturdy, interlocking pyramids of carbon atoms. The pyramid is among the strongest structures in nature, which is what gives the diamond its hardness and indestructibility. Their structure (especially once cut into a multifaceted stone) is ideally suited for dispersing visible white light into its component colors. The sparkle or brilliance of diamonds makes them prized jewelry. Diamonds are also commonly used to make blades for cutting and drilling.

Water is made up of hydrogen and oxygen atoms and contains no carbon. (See earth science bonus question.)

Iron is a heavy metallic element used in construction, tools, and armament.

Oxalates are organic (or carbon-containing) chemicals found in certain plant foods that can combine with calcium to form calcium oxalate, a mildly toxic chemical that the body does not use.

35. At room temperature, some elements are gas, some are liquid, but most are _____.

Solid.

At room temperature and pressure, almost all elements are solids, although two are liquids. Eleven elements are gases: the noble gases (helium, neon, argon, krypton, xenon, and radon), hydrogen, oxygen, nitrogen, fluorine, and chlorine. All the rest are solids, including the metals (such as iron, zinc, nickel, and platinum) and nonmetals (such as sulfur and iodine). (See question 39.)

36. When heated, how does the volume of a gas change?

It expands.

The effect of temperature on the motion of molecules is one of the most important concepts for physics students. The unique property of a gas is that its molecules are not attached to each other in any way. Each molecule is free and is able to move. The speed at which a typical gas molecule moves is several hundred kilometers per hour. Distance between the molecules is also very large compared to the size of the molecules themselves. Two other key properties of a gas are that it has no definite volume and no definite shape. Gas always takes both the volume and the shape of the container it is placed in. If a gas is not in a container, it will spread out as far as it possibly can.

Heating a gas will cause thermal expansion, which means the molecules move faster and farther apart. An experiment to imitate the heat movement of gas particles and thus understand their energy would be to put some small stones in a tin with a lid. Replace the lid and shake the tin. You can feel and hear the stones rattling inside the tin. The stones are knocking against the walls of the tin. If you shake much harder, the stones may knock the lid off the tin and burst out. The movement of gas particles in a closed container is similar to the movement of the stones. If you heat the gas particles they move faster and can burst the closed container. Thus, heating a liquid or a gas in a closed container can be very dangerous.

37. An atom is made up of protons, neutrons, and

_____.

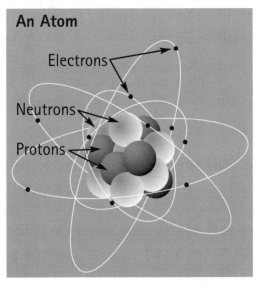

An Atom

Electrons

Neutrons

Protons

Electrons.

The building block of all matter, including molecules, is the atom. It is the smallest unit an element can be broken down to, and is made up of subatomic particles known as protons, electrons, and neutrons. At the center of the atom is a nucleus, which is usually surrounded by one or more negatively charged electrons moving in orbit around it. The nucleus is positively charged and contains one or more of the relatively heavy particles known as protons and neutrons. A proton is positively charged, while a neutron has no charge. The number of protons in the nucleus of an atom defines that element's atomic number, which can be found by looking up the element in the periodic table. (See questions 33 and 40.)

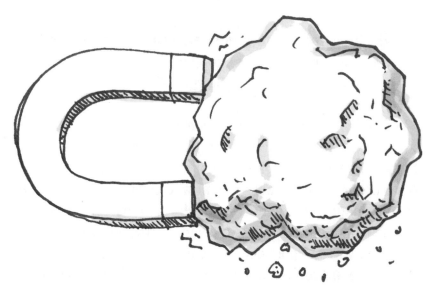

38. Where are most metals naturally found?
    a) in decaying trees   c) in the stratosphere
    b) in the ground   d) in flowing rivers

About 75 percent of the periodic table is made up of different kinds of metals. Metals are solid at normal temperatures, are good conductors of heat and electricity, and are very reactive. They are also usually opaque (meaning you can't see through them). We often find metals naturally in the form of ores, which are minerals or rocks that can contain metals. Valuable ores, such as iron, silver, and gold, are mined, after which the other metals are extracted for human purposes.

Man used metals as early as 1100 BC. This fact is based on the dating of a copper mining site in Cyprus, including artifacts of bronze and iron. Around 750 BC the Chinese developed cast iron; while iron was used before this time, no one had produced the high temperatures necessary to melt it. By using charcoal, the Chinese succeeded in melting iron, casting it with molds, and making tools, vessels, and artwork. Today, metals are used for everything from buildings and bridges to electronics and common tools like hammers.

39. Which one of the following elements is not a metal?
　　a) mercury　　　　c) copper
　　b) sodium　　　　**d) sulfur** 👉

    Sulfur is not a metal. It is a chemical element consisting of sixteen neutrons, sixteen electrons, and sixteen protons. Its atomic number is 16. Nonmetals are the elements in groups 14–16 of the periodic table. Chemical elements, such as sulfur, cannot conduct electricity or heat very well. As opposed to metals, nonmetallic elements are very brittle, and cannot be rolled into wires or pounded into sheets. Aside from the noble gases, there are seven nonmetal elements: hydrogen, oxygen, carbon, nitrogen, phosphorus, sulfur, and selenium. These elements exist in two of the three states of matter at room temperature: gas (such as oxygen) and solid (such as carbon). Sulfur has no metallic luster, and does not reflect light.

    Mercury is the only metal that is liquid at ordinary temperatures. Mercury is sometimes called quicksilver. It is a heavy, silvery-white liquid metal that was once used in thermometers, thermostats, and dental fillings. Its atomic number is 80. (See Chemistry bonus question.)

    Sodium is most often thought of in terms of nutrition. Its most common compound is sodium chloride, or ordinary table salt, which is necessary to many forms of life. Its atomic number is 11. It is classified as a metal because it conducts electricity, and it has the silvery, metallic sheen common to all metals.

    Copper is an important metal. It is malleable, and a good conductor of heat and electricity (second only to silver in electrical conductivity). Its alloys, brass and bronze, are also very useful. Its atomic number is 29. (See following question.)

40. Every element has an atomic mass. What does this number represent?

The average mass of an element's atoms.

The mass of an atom is expressed in atomic mass units (amu) and is roughly equal to the number of protons plus the number of neutrons of that element. This is because both the protons and the neutrons in an atom have a relatively equal mass. The mass of an electron is so insignificant that it does not need to be included. An element's atomic mass is often found beneath the particular element's symbol in its box in the periodic table of elements. (See questions 33 and 37.)

41. The way we express the time it takes for atoms in a radioactive substance to disintegrate is called:
a) entropy.   c) inertia.
b) decomposition.   d) half-life.

Half-life is the time it takes for half of the atoms in a sample of radioactive material to disintegrate, or decay. During this chemical decomposition, one substance is broken down into two or more simpler ones. (However, while half the material decays in one half-life, all of it does not decay in two half-lives.) For each particular substance, this time varies. Scientists have determined half-lives through years of experimentation. Knowing the half-life of something can help us determine how to safely store such products as nuclear waste.

Radioactive decay is also used for carbon dating. All natural materials contain carbon 14, a radioactive version of normal carbon. This begins to decay at a known rate, so determining the amount of C-14 allows scientists to determine the age of things.

Egyptian mummies, sunken boats, and other ancient artifacts have all been dated using this technique.

Entropy is a way to measure the dispersal of energy in a process in our material world.

Decomposition is when something is broken down into smaller parts.

Inertia is the resistance an object has to a change its state of motion. (See question 46.)

42. Fire needs _____ to continue burning.
  a) oil   **c) paper or wood**
  b) wind   **<u>d) oxygen</u>**

Fire is a chemical chain reaction that involves heat, fuel, and oxygen. If any one of these three elements is removed, the fire can no longer burn. Fire uses oxygen and combines it with elements in the fuel (often carbon) to produce smoky gases (such as carbon dioxide or carbon monoxide) that are dangerous, and sometimes poisonous to human beings in large amounts. Firefighters usually use water to extinguish fires, but another technique is to deprive the fire of oxygen.

Although fire and smoke can be dangerous, in controlled situations both have been useful to humans. Among other things, humans have used fire for light, for cooking, for heat, and to make weapons and tools. Smoke was used by American Indians to signal each other over long distances. Fire is often given much credit as an essential factor in the rise of human civilization.

43. What happens over time when iron is exposed to oxygen?

It rusts.

Rust is the common name for a very common compound, iron oxide. For iron (chemical symbol Fe) to become iron oxide, three things are required: iron, water, and oxygen. Iron oxide, (Fe_2O_3) is so common because iron readily combines with oxygen (so readily, in fact, that pure iron is only rarely found in nature). Iron or steel rusting is an example of corrosion, an electrochemical process. Water speeds the process because it allows for the formation of hydroxide (OH^-) ions. The rust that forms is much weaker than iron; when iron becomes severely rusted, it will crumble away.

To prevent rusting (or the oxidation of iron), rustproof paint can be applied—a common occurrence on the Golden Gate Bridge in San Francisco. In other applications, nickel and chromium are added to iron to bind together the atoms and prevent them from rusting.

44. What happens when you combine baking soda and vinegar?

It fizzes.

Mixing an acid and base together creates a powerful reaction. A safe way to test this reaction is to take a teaspoon of vinegar and put it into a large glass. Then add a pinch of baking soda. Bubbles will come up from the vinegar as it reacts with the baking soda. This is because vinegar is an acid, and baking soda is a base, so they neutralize each other, creating salts, water, and carbon dioxide gas. The carbon dioxide gas is what makes the vinegar bubble.

People often use this mixture as a simple, nontoxic drain cleaner, to unclog their drains. They pour the mixture down the drain, cover it with the stopper, and the gas that is created forces any particles down the drain.

45. What is the difference between a chemical change and a physical change?

A chemical change is any change to a chemical bond, which is the bond that holds atoms together in a molecule. Here are some examples:

- iron rusting (iron oxide is formed)
- gasoline burning (water vapor, carbon dioxide, and pollutants are formed)
- eggs cooking (a network is formed when fluid protein molecules uncoil and cross-link)
- bread rising (carbon dioxide gas is created when yeast acts on carbohydrates)

• milk souring (sour-tasting lactic acid is produced)
• skin tanning from the sun (vitamin D and melanin are produced)

Physical change rearranges molecules, but it doesn't affect their internal structures. Some examples of physical change are:

• whipping egg whites (air is forced into the fluid, but no new substance is produced)
• magnetizing a compass needle (iron atoms are realigned, but no real change occurs within the iron atoms themselves)
• boiling water (water molecules are forced away from each other when the liquid changes to vapor, but their chemical formula, H_2O, does not change)
• dissolving sugar in water (sugar molecules are dispersed throughout the water, but the individual sugar molecules are unchanged)

Physics
Answers

46. Sir Isaac Newton taught us that for every action (or force), there is an equal and opposite _____.

Reaction force.

Newton's third law of motion states, "for every action, there is an equal and opposite reaction." For any force (action) one object exerts upon a second object, there is a reaction force applied by the second object back onto the first object. This reaction force is always equal in magnitude and opposite in direction from the action force. For example, if you hit a ball with a baseball bat, the bat exerts a force on the ball as it hits it. At the same time, the ball exerts an equal but opposite force on the bat. The same concept applies in soccer (a player may lose his balance after a kick) and in car accidents (in which one car hits another or when a car hits another object). (For more about Sir Isaac Newton, see questions 2 and 50.)

47. If an object is moving, it has energy. What do we call this energy?

Kinetic energy.

The energy of motion is called kinetic energy (k). Kinetic energy is measured by how much work is needed to either put an object from rest into its current state of motion, or to bring a moving object to rest. The more mass (m) an object has, and the greater its velocity (v), the greater the object's kinetic energy. To determine something's kinetic energy, we use the equation $k=1/2mv^2$. In other words, the kinetic energy of an object is one-half of its mass times its velocity squared.

48. Name a machine that operates without any external power source.

None exist.

There is no machine that operates without any external power source. Such a machine, commonly referred to as a perpetual motion machine, has been attempted by many over the years, but no one has succeeded. Even Leonardo da Vinci failed to invent one. People's attempts have included all sorts of components, such as a wheel of revolving balls, magnets, pulleys, and ramps. Such a machine would defy the law of conservation of energy, one of the most fundamental of all natural laws. No system can produce more energy than is supplied to it.

49. At the same pressure, which is more dense—hot air or cold air?

Cold air.

Cold air is more dense than warm air. Air is made up of nitrogen, oxygen, and other molecules that are moving around at incredible speeds, colliding with each other and all other objects. The higher the temperature is, the faster the molecules move. As the air is heated, the molecules speed up and push harder against their surroundings and each other. If the volume of the area is not fixed, this increases the space between the molecules, making the air less dense. For example, when the air in a hot-air balloon is heated, it expands (molecules speed up and spread apart). Now less dense than the surrounding air, the balloon rises. When the heater is turned off, the air in the balloon cools, the molecules slow down and move closer together, and the balloon descends. (See question 36.)

50. Who discovered the relationship between energy (E), mass (m), and the speed of light (c), as expressed in the equation E=mc²?

   a) Marie Curie   **c) Albert Einstein**
   b) Louis Pasteur   **d) Sir Isaac Newton**

Albert Einstein (1879–1955) was born in Germany, and lived in various parts of Europe before moving to the United States in 1933 to escape the Nazi government. In 1905, Einstein announced what has become probably the most famous theory in science, his special theory of relativity, including the famous equation $E=mc^2$. The equation states that neither mass nor energy are conserved separately, but instead can be traded for one another, and only the total mass-energy is conserved. In the equation, m equals mass; c, which stands for constant, equals the speed of light (186,000 miles per second, or 299,338 km per second); and E equals the resulting energy equivalent of the mass. Because the speed of light squared is a very large number when expressed in appropriate units, a small amount of mass corresponds to a huge amount of energy. (For more on Albert Einstein, see question 100.)

Polish-born scientist Marie Curie (1867–1934) discovered radioactivity, and the element radium, and was the first person to ever win two Nobel prizes.

Louis Pasteur (1822–1895) was born in France, and established that most infectious diseases are caused by germs (e.g., bacteria, viruses, fungi, and protozoans). This idea became the foundation of microbiology and the cornerstone of modern medicine. (See question 19.)

Sir Isaac Newton (1642–1727) was from England. He discovered the law of gravity, invented the reflecting telescope, and established the three laws of motion now known as Newton's laws. He is also known for his discovery of differential and integral calculus, which were also (independently) discovered by Gottfried Wilhelm Leibniz.

51. Name two of the three forces that act on objects without touching them.

Magnetic, electrical, and gravitational.

Magnetic force is the force exerted between magnetic poles. These poles can be Earth's magnetic poles or the poles (opposite ends) of a magnet. The farther away the magnetic poles are from each other, the weaker the strength of the magnetic force field. Magnetic force manifests itself primarily with the element iron, but it is also associated with electric currents and moving electrically charged particles. Because of this, it is related to electrical force. (See question 52.)

Electrical force is exerted by objects with charge. There are two kinds of electrical charges—positive (+) and negative (-). Like charges (e.g., + and +) repel each other, while opposite charges (+ and -) attract each other. Electrical forces were first observed by the Greeks, who found that, after being rubbed with fur, pieces of amber (in Greek, *elektron*) attracted other objects.

Gravitational force is the attraction between masses, believed to be a universal force. It is what keeps the planets orbiting the sun, and the moon orbiting Earth.

52. What keeps the planets orbiting around the sun, and makes things fall to the ground?

Gravity.

Because the sun is so immense (about 330,000 times more massive than Earth), its gravity provides a centripetal, or center-seeking, force that keeps the planets in orbit. Imagine that there is a string going from the sun to Earth. Earth wants to move in a straight line, but the imaginary string (or gravitational pull) keeps pulling Earth toward the sun. The result is neither a line nor a circle, but an ellipse. If this gravitational pull were disconnected, Earth would move off in a straight line, at a constant speed, away from the sun. The moon, and satellites orbiting Earth, act in the exact same manner due to the centripetal force of gravity.

Gravity acts in a similar way with matter on Earth's surface. When you are standing on the surface of the planet, there is a force of gravity acting upon you. Earth is a much, much larger mass than you, and its gravity overpowers your inertia and pulls you toward its center. This keeps you on the ground, instead of spinning off into space. You stay at the surface because the surface pushes against you, exactly balancing the force of gravity that pulls you down. It is this force opposing gravity that causes you to feel weight, and why in space you are weightless. (See question 51.)

53. What color would you see if you were to shine a red, blue, and yellow light on the same place on a white piece of paper?

You would see the color white.

Although a color spectrum shows a continuous range of colors, the human eye only has receptors (called cones) for three primary additive colors—red, blue, and yellow. Our minds perceive a particular color based on how much each kind of cone is stimulated by the light hitting small regions on our retinas. Any color we see, including white, can be created by mixing various intensities of the three additive primary colors. Gray and white are created by mixing the exact same amount of each of the three primary colors.

What would happen if you were to mix these colors using paint instead of light? If you guessed a dark brown or black, you are right. Why the difference? We see the light reflecting off of paper. The dyes in paint are subtractive, absorbing certain colors and reflecting the leftover colors. In subtractive colors, there are also three primary colors: red, blue, and yellow. Gray and black are produced by mixing the primary subtractive colors together in equal quantities.

Interestingly, other animals have different types or amounts of cones in their retinas than humans. Therefore, these animals perceive different primary colors. This also means that on an RGB (Red-Green-Blue) screen, like a computer screen, what looks to a human like a perfect color photo of a flower might look entirely different to other animals.

54. Name some imaging techniques that allow you to see something you wouldn't be able to see with just your eyes.

Ultrasound, electromagnetic radiation, and MRI.

Ultrasound, or sonography, uses high-frequency sound waves to view internal areas of a body, such as internal tissues and organs, blood flow, and heart-valve functions, or to view the fetus in a pregnant woman.

Electromagnetic radiation can be used to form images including x-rays, CAT scans, and infrared energy. X-rays use invisible, highly penetrating electromagnetic radiation at a higher frequency than visible light. Doctors use x-ray machines to produce a visual image of a body's bone and organ structures. CAT scans (computerized axial tomography) are an expanded form of x-rays, taking several pictures of the body from different angles, and creating cross-sections of tissues, organs, and bone with great clarity. Infrared imaging uses heat or thermal radiation in much the same way as a camera uses light. The result is a thermal "map" of the object.

MRI machines (magnetic resonance imaging) use magnets in conjunction with radio-wave pulses to create images so detailed that they can show blood flowing in virtually every part of the body.

55. How would you make a sonic boom?

By traveling faster than sound.

A sonic boom is caused by an object, usually an aircraft, moving faster than sound—about 750 miles (1,207 km) per hour at sea level. An aircraft traveling through the atmosphere continuously produces air-pressure waves similar to the water waves caused by a ship's bow. When the aircraft exceeds the speed of sound, these pressure waves combine and form shock waves that are heard on the ground as sonic booms. A sonic boom is defined as the sudden onset and release of pressure after the buildup by the shock wave. Sonic booms typically are heard at ground level two to sixty seconds after the plane flies over, depending on the altitude of the aircraft.

Brigadier General Chuck Yeager, flying his specially made plane, the Bell X-1 (which he called the Glamorous Glennis), created the first man-made sonic boom in 1947. More recently, the Concorde, an extremely fast jet, flew fast enough on a transatlantic flight to create sonic booms. The plane made the voyage in much less time than traditional planes. However, the first true man-made sonic boom is much simpler than either of those—the cracking sound made by the tip of a whip is actually a small sonic boom.

56. Why is walking on ice or driving on wet roads so difficult?

There is very little friction.

Friction is the resistance to motion when one surface comes into contact with and rubs against another surface. Although two objects might look smooth, they are actually rough and jagged when viewed with a microscope. As they slide against each other, they grind and drag against the roughness of each other's surfaces, creating friction and preventing slipping. Friction also creates heat, and can wear down surfaces or slow down engines. To reduce the effects of friction, substances like oil or silicone can be used as lubrication, making the parts slippery. For example, when you oil a squeaky hinge, the oil works to reduce the surface roughness by filling in the tiny cracks so that the pieces stop rubbing together as much, and the noise lessens.

Ice, rain, or oil on a surface reduce friction, causing you to slip when walking, climbing, or driving. When sand is spread on an icy road, it adds friction by making the surface rougher, making it less slippery for tires.

57. We get energy to heat and cool our homes and run machines from many sources. Name as many sources of energy as you can.

Sun, wind, wood, fossil fuels, water, natural gas, geothermal activity, and nuclear fission.

1. Sun: The sun is the most inexhaustible and cleanest source of energy. Solar energy is collected and stored via solar panels that face the sun to collect solar radiation during daylight hours. The challenge of solar energy is the large expense of making the panels. (See general science bonus question.)

2. Wind: Humans have used wind as a primary source of energy for centuries, such as in propelling sailing ships or powering windmills. Wind is caused by the cyclical heating and cooling of the earth's atmosphere by sunlight and shadow, and by flow of air from high to low pressure regions, and perhaps by other factors, too. However, it has two major drawbacks in terms of energy use: storage and unreliability.

3. Wood: Wood and other organic materials (such as plant products like cornhusks, wastepaper, and cow dung) can be burned, fermented, or chemically treated to release energy. Although wood and other materials are an inexpensive source of heat and energy, they give off smoke and pollution, and are in limited supply.

4. Fossil fuels: Fossil fuels are sources of energy found inside the earth that have been there for millions of years. Both coal and petroleum are fossil fuels. Coal is a rock that releases energy as it burns. It is mostly made of the chemical element carbon. The greater the concentration of carbon in the coal, the higher its potential energy. Petroleum, or oil, is formed of the decayed plants and animals that lived millions of years

ago. Fossil fuels are nonrenewable, meaning that once we use up all we have, no more can be obtained.

5. Water: Hydropower, obtained by harnessing moving water, produces about 20 percent of the world's electricity. In the United States, hydropower accounts for about 12 percent of the nation's supply of electricity, and over 90 percent of all electricity that comes from renewable resources. Hydropower is created by collecting water in dammed lakes, streams, and rivers. The water funnels through the dam, into a powerhouse, and turns a large wheel or turbine, that then creates electricity via a generator. Dams can have negative consequences on the environment, however, by interfering in the lives of animals that live in the rivers. (See earth science bonus question.)

6. Natural gas: Natural gas is made up mostly of methane, a combination of hydrogen and carbon that is composed of long-dead plants and tiny animals. Millions of years ago, these organisms died and were buried along with mud and sand, usually on floors of lakes, oceans, and riverbeds. Over time, bacteria broke down the buried organic matter and created methane gas. This gas is tapped and processed to provide heat and energy.

7. Geothermal energy: Geothermal energy is harnessed from the earth's natural heat found deep inside both active and recently inactivated volcanoes. Steam from high-temperature geothermal fluids is used to drive turbines and generate electrical power, while low-temperature fluids provide hot water for home heating, greenhouses, industrial factories, and hot springs. Geothermal heat is renewable, and a cleaner source of energy than fossil fuels or wood. In Iceland, many homes are heated almost entirely with this kind of energy.

8. Nuclear: The principle of producing electricity by heat is the same in nuclear-power production as in coal- or petroleum-

based energy production. Water is boiled to create high-pressure steam, which in turn rotates a turbine. The generator attached to the turbine generates electricity. In a nuclear-power plant, the heat needed to boil the steam and rotate the turbine is generated by a nuclear reactor through the fission (or breaking apart) of atomic nuclei. Current forms of nuclear-power production create radioactive waste products that require centuries to become safe.

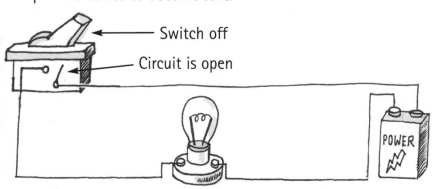

Switch off

Circuit is open

POWER

58. When you flip on a light switch, the light turns on. Why?

The electric circuit through the light bulb is closed.

A circuit contains a source of electric current and conducting materials (such as wires) arranged in a loop. When the light switch is turned on, the loop is continuous, or closed, and electricity can flow through the circuit and power the light. If the light is an incandescent bulb, the electricity flows through the bulb's filament, which heats up so much it becomes white-hot. It is the light given off by the filament that you see when you turn on the light. When the switch is turned off, the loop is broken by the switch and so no current can flow to power the bulb. A circuit that is broken is said to be open.

59. How can you use a lemon to light a light bulb?

Turn the lemon into a battery.

A lemon can be used like a battery by placing a copper penny and a steel paper clip (or a zinc-coated nail) into slits cut into the lemon skin, then connecting the penny and clip with a small piece of wire. The two different metals react with the acid in the lemon juice and cause electrons to travel from the negative terminal (the steel or zinc) to the positive terminal (the penny). An electric potential is created when the different metals are immersed in the lemon, and you can measure this with a voltmeter. One lemon alone will probably not produce enough power to light a bulb, but if you link four or more lemons together in a circuit by connecting the negative terminal of one lemon to the positive terminal of the next, and so on, you may get enough electricity to light an LED bulb, or some other small device.

60. What is an efficient way to convert electrical current into light that generates almost no heat?

Using a light-emitting diode (LED).

Light-emitting diodes, or LEDs, are used in a variety of ways: They light up your watch or digital alarm clock; they send information from your remote control; and they signal that your camera or hand-held video game is working correctly. They can also be used in big-screen TVs, traffic lights, and flashlights. You also see them as small lights showing whether a machine is turned on or off. An LED is a tiny light bulb, but it doesn't have a wire filament like typical light bulbs. LEDs light up via the movement of electrons in semiconductor material. This movement causes the release of photons, the most basic unit of light. The main advantage of LEDs is that they are very efficient. While regular incandescent light bulbs get very hot, LEDs barely release any heat. Unlike lightbulbs, LEDs last for a very long time, which makes them especially useful in places that are hard to access.

61. How does a semiconductor work?

By conducting electric impulses in a controlled fashion.

Semiconductors have had a monumental impact on our society. You find semiconductors inside most microprocessor chips—the heart of any normal computer. Anything that's computerized or uses radio waves depends on semiconductors.

Semiconductors, often created with silicon, allow the transmission and control of electric impulses in microscopic circuits. The smallness of these circuits has led to portable technology that could not have been built with the previous technology of vacuum tubes. For example, the computing power of a modern laptop computer would have required a large building full of power-hungry equipment and a large maintenance staff were it not for semiconductor technology.

A diode is the simplest possible semiconductor device, and is therefore an excellent beginning point if you want to understand how semiconductors work. A diode allows current to flow in one direction but not the other. You may have seen turnstiles at a stadium that let people go through in only one direction. A diode is a one-way turnstile for electrons. Most diodes are made from silicon. You can change the behavior of silicon and turn it into a conductor by mixing a small amount of an impurity into the silicon crystal. A minute amount of an impurity turns a silicon crystal into a viable, but not great, conductor—hence the name "semiconductor."

62. Why is the sound of an approaching ambulance different from the sound of an ambulance going away from you?

The Doppler effect.

The Doppler effect, or Doppler shift, is the change in the wavelength (or frequency) of waves as a result of the motion of either the source or receiver. If the source of the waves and the receiver are approaching each other, the frequency of the waves will increase, the wavelength will be shortened and the sounds will become higher pitched.

If the sender and receiver are moving away from each other, the frequency of the sound waves will decrease and the wavelength will be lengthened, thus causing the sounds to become lower pitched. This effect is named for the Austrian scientist, Christian Doppler (1803–1853), who demonstrated the Doppler effect for sound.

63. If you were to build a bridge out of a pile of stones, the shape you would create is a called_____.

An arch.

By placing the stones in the shape of an arch, the weight of the stones is distributed all along the arch to the abutments—where the bridge touches the ground. This means there is almost no tension on the underside of the bridge, making it a very stable design. It can even be built without any mortar; the stones will stay standing due to the exertion of force that one stone has on another. This force is caused by the equal pressure gravity puts on each stone. The Romans built arch-shaped bridges and aqueducts that are still standing today.

64. If you had two crowns, one of pure gold and one of gold mixed with silver, how could you tell them apart without using a scale or destroying them?

By submerging them in water.

Solid gold is denser than gold mixed with silver, so you can easily tell the difference between a gold crown and an alloy crown (one made of mixed metals) by its density. It is hard to measure the volume of a complicated shape like a crown, but there is an easy method. The story often told is that Archimedes, a Greek physicist, mathematician, and inventor, figured out the solution to this puzzle while in his bathtub.

He developed what is now called Archimedes's Principle, which states that a body immersed in a fluid is buoyed up by a force equal to the weight of the displaced fluid. This means that if an object is less dense than a fluid it is in, it will float. If it is denser, it will sink. Helium balloons float in air and boats float in water because they are less dense than the surrounding fluid.

So both crowns will sink in a pot of water because silver and gold are both more dense than water. One way to measure the volume of a crown would be to note the initial height of the water, drop the crown in, and then measure the volume of water to be removed to get the water back to its initial height. The denser solid gold crown will have a greater ratio of weight to volume.

65. The quickest way to cool a bottle of soda is to place it:
a) in a bucket of ice.
☞ **b) in a bucket of ice water.**
c) in a bucket of extremely cold water with no ice.
d) outside on the porch when it is very cold.

A bottle of soda will cool most quickly in a bucket of ice water because more of its surface area is touching the colder liquid, allowing more heat to leave the soda and enter the ice water. If the bottle were just in a bucket of ice, less of the bottle would touch the ice, and the cooling would not be as fast. It will also cool faster than if it were outside because water is a more effective conductor of heat than air.

66. Why does it hurt so much when you hit the water jumping into a swimming pool?

Because you are breaking the surface tension.

In a liquid, the molecules have a strong enough attraction to one another to keep them from flying apart. At a boundary between the liquid and air, the molecules crowd closer together than inside the liquid, and so the attraction creates a kind of skin over the water, called surface tension. This is why it can be painful when you hit the water, especially from high up. Your body is hitting that skin, and it has to break through the clinging molecules. Belly-flopping hurts because you are breaking the surface tension over a large region of water all at once. In a dive, you break the surface tension with a small, sharp surface made by your hands. As a result, the force is small. (The amount of force is surface tension times the horizontal area of your body hitting the water.) The height from which you jump makes a difference as well; the higher the diving board, the faster you will be going when you hit the water, and therefore the harder you will hit it.

A way to see the clinging power of water molecules is to use an eyedropper to drip water slowly onto a penny. After a number of drops, the water will begin to bulge over the edges of the penny, but it won't drip off because surface tension holds it together. Eventually, if you keep adding drops, the water will run off. How many drops of water do you think can remain on the surface of a penny before the water runs off?

Water striders, a kind of insect, use surface tension to stand on and move across the surface of ponds and lakes. They are light enough that while their legs make little dents in the surface tension they don't break through.

67. What was one of the things that helped Ludwig van Beethoven compose music even though he was deaf?

He felt the vibrations of the music through the floor.

All sound, whether it is the noise from a truck on the highway or a rock band at a concert, is a vibration. Just like light is a wave of photons, sound is a wave of matter. The molecules vibrate back and forth along the path the sound is traveling, producing a wave. This wave, and its varying frequencies, is what transmits sound. This is why the floor can feel like it is shaking when you listen to loud music with a lot of low notes.

Beethoven, before he became a composer, was a virtuoso pianist. However, as he slowly lost his hearing and finally became fully deaf, he lost his ability to perform. It was then that he began to compose. He was able to continue writing music in part because of the extensive musical knowledge he already possessed, but also because, by removing the legs from his piano so that both he and the piano were directly on the floor, he could feel the vibrations of the music and "hear" what it sounded like. (For more about the properties of sound, see question 62.)

Earth Science Answers

68. When astronauts look at Earth from outer space, the planet looks blue. Why?

Vast amounts of water.

Earth's color comes from reflected, absorbed, transmitted, and scattered sunlight. Sunlight contains all the colors of the spectrum, but it interacts differently with air, land, plants, and water. Natural land (soil, rocks, and sand) tends to be primarily brown or gray. This is because these colors are reflected; all the others are absorbed. Trees and grasses tend to be green because the green part of sunlight is reflected.

Water is trickier. Sunlight first enters Earth's atmosphere, where air molecules scatter the blue part of light best. Then the sunlight itself and the scattered sunlight both reach the ocean, lake, or river surfaces. Barring things in the water like algae, mud, or pollution, the blue part of light is most easily reflected by the water. It is this blue light that astronauts see from space. (For more on light reflection, see question 88.)

Since water covers about 70 percent, or a total of 139.5 million square miles (224.5 million square km), of the planet's surface, Earth appears like a big blue marble against the blackness of outer space.

69. Each year, Earth revolves once around what?

☞ **(a) the sun**   (c) its axis
   (b) the moon   (d) the Milky Way

Earth's orbit around the sun is called Earth revolution. This celestial motion takes 365.26 days to complete one cycle. Earth's orbit around the sun is not circular, but elliptical. An elliptical orbit causes the distance from Earth to the sun to vary annually. Because Earth's axis is tilted in relation to its orbit, the Northern Hemisphere receives longer and more direct exposure to the sun for half the year. For the other half, the Southern Hemisphere receives the warmer weather. (See question 70.)

The moon revolves around Earth much in the same way that Earth revolves around the sun, but it takes only 28 days for the moon's revolution.

Earth's axis is the invisible line extending through its center from pole to pole. Earth spins, or rotates, on its axis one rotation every twenty-four hours, causing day and night.

The Milky Way is the galaxy to which our solar system belongs. (See question 72.)

70. Is a lunar year longer or shorter than a solar year?

Shorter.

A lunar year is eleven days shorter than a solar year. A solar year is 365.26 days, the amount of time it takes for Earth to revolve around the sun. In the same way Earth revolves around the sun, the moon revolves around Earth. If Earth were not revolving around the sun, the moon would revolve around Earth every 28 days. But, because Earth is moving, the moon has to "catch up." To get back to the same place for a new or full moon, the moon has to travel an additional 1.5 days. This makes a lunar month—the time from new moon to new moon—29 days, 12 hours, and 44 minutes long.

Some religions, such as Christianity, have a solar calendar so that their holidays stay seasonally based and occur at or around the same time every year. A good example of this is Easter, which falls on a different date every year but always occurs in the spring. The civil calendar, used around the world, is also a solar calendar. It is based on Earth's progression around the sun, and so is constant each year.

Other religions, such as Islam and Buddhism, follow a lunar calendar. The holidays shift 11 days earlier each year, so a holiday in the spring would be in the winter a decade later. Judaism has a lunar calendar with a solar correction so that the dates of holidays shift but they never change seasons.

71. The sun is a:
    (a) planet.   (c) star. 🖝
    (b) meteor.   (d) reflection.

The sun is not only a star; it is the only star in our solar system. It is also quite large. The surface of the sun is 109 times larger than Earth, and its interior could hold over 1.3 million Earths. The sun's outer visible layer is called the photosphere and has a temperature of about 11,000°F (6,000°C). This layer has a mottled appearance when viewed from Earth or space through telescopes due to the turbulent eruptions of energy at the surface. Solar energy is created deep within the core of the sun.

Planets are celestial bodies (other than comets or satellites) that revolve (or orbit) around a sun in a solar system. In our solar system, there are nine confirmed planets—in order going outward from the sun, they are Mercury, Venus, Earth, Mars, Jupiter, Saturn, Uranus, Neptune, and Pluto. (See question 72 and the general science bonus question.)

A meteor is a bright streak that appears in the sky when a meteoroid enters Earth's atmosphere and is heated by friction with air molecules.

Reflection occurs when light bounces off a surface. (See question 88.)

72. How many planets are in our solar system? Which one is closest to the sun?

Nine (maybe ten*); Mercury is closest to the sun.

Mercury is the closest planet to the sun, and the second-smallest planet in the solar system. Its diameter is 40 percent smaller than Earth's and 40 percent larger than the moon's. Venus is the next planet from the sun. Its orbit is the closest of any planet to being a perfect circle, and it is often the brightest object in the sky apart from the sun and the moon. After Venus comes Earth, and then Mars. Mars is often called "the red planet" because its surface is composed of red dirt. Mars has a very thin atmosphere and is therefore much colder, on average, than Earth would be at the same distance from the sun. Jupiter, the next planet, is by far the largest; it is twice as massive as all the other planets combined and 318 times as massive as Earth. Saturn comes next, and is surrounded by impressive rings composed of innumerable particles, each with an individual orbit. They range in size from a few centimeters to a few meters, with a few as big as several kilometers. Uranus, Saturn's neighbor, has a distinct blue appearance, which comes from the absorption of red light by the methane in its atmosphere. Neptune, the next planet, has an internal heat source (as do Saturn and Jupiter); it radiates more than twice the energy it receives from the sun. Pluto, the last confirmed planet, has an extremely irregular orbit. Sometimes it crosses that of Neptune and becomes the eighth-farthest from the sun for several years.

*It has been long agreed upon that there were nine planets in our solar system. However, advances in technology have made more precise observations possible. In 2005, scientists discovered what is believed to be another planet. Larger than Pluto, it is about ninety-seven times as far away from the sun as Earth. Its temporary name is 2003 UB313 (a permanent, more catchy name is awaiting confirmation that it is, indeed, a new planet in our solar system).

Ozone Layer

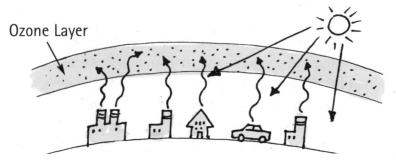

73. What is the name of the layer of the atmosphere that protects us from the sun's harmful rays?

The ozone layer.

The ozone layer, or ozonosphere, is one of many layers surrounding the earth. The layer closest to the earth is the troposphere (where our weather occurs) and it extends from the earth's surface to altitudes of 5-10 miles (8-16 km) high. It is thinner near the poles and thicker near the equator.

The stratosphere lies above the troposphere and is dry and less dense. The temperature of this region is actually warmer than the upper levels of the troposphere due to the absorption of ultraviolet radiation. The ozone layer, which absorbs and scatters the solar ultraviolet radiation, is in this layer. Ninety-nine percent of the earth's atmosphere is located in the troposphere and stratosphere.

The stratosphere contains relatively high concentrations of ozone, located at altitudes of 12-30 miles (19-48 km) above the earth's surface. Ozone is formed when solar ultraviolet light interacts with oxygen. Instead of two oxygen molecules joining to make O_2, three join to make O_3.

The ozone layer prevents most ultraviolet (UV) and other high-energy radiation from penetrating the earth's surface, but does allow sufficient UV rays through to activate vitamin D in humans. However, the full radiation, if not weakened by this filtering effect of ozone, would destroy animal tissue. Higher levels of radiation resulting from the depletion of the ozone layer have been linked with illnesses such as skin cancer, and are even thought to cause the death of certain amphibian species.

74. Gravitational pull from the moon causes shifts in bodies of water. What are these shifts called?

Tides.

Tides are governed by the relative position of the moon and the sun, both of which exert a gravitational pull. This pull attracts the waters of Earth toward them, creating tides all over the planet. The rising tide is called a flood (from the thirteenth century English sailors' word *flod*) and the falling tide is called an ebb. There are two high tides and two low tides every twenty-five hours, linked to Earth's rotation on its axis.

The sun exerts a gravitational pull 180 times as strong as the moon's gravitational pull on Earth, but the variation in the moon's force is more than two times larger than the variation in the sun's force because it is so much closer to Earth. Because of this, it is the lunar effect that creates the major variance in tides. The highest tides in the world are found in Canada's Bay of Fundy. Caused by the bay's unique shape and other factors, the tides are much more dramatic than anywhere else in the world. (For more about gravity, see question 52.)

75. What are the three measurements we need to determine the exact location of a place?

Longitude, latitude, and height coordinates.

On the globe, imaginary lines of longitude (or meridians) run from pole to pole like the segments of an orange. To determine the distance from meridian to meridian means making an east to west circular path around the earth. These lines make rings or circles, containing 360 degrees of measurement, and are known as latitude lines. They run parallel to the equator.

The meridian passing through the Royal Astronomical Observatory in Greenwich, England, is zero longitude and is known as the prime meridian. Longitude is measured from 0 to 180 degrees east and west. The 180° meridian is the same for both east and west and is found in the western Pacific Ocean. The international date line lies near and along this longitude line.

Latitude lines describe the distance from the equator either north or south latitude. The latitude of the equator is zero degrees, while the poles are at 90 degrees north and south. At the poles, the latitude lines become a point and lie at right angles to the equatorial plane.

Using longitude and latitude coordinates, one can pinpoint any location on the surface of the earth. These coordinates are actually angles divided into degrees and "minutes of arc" and "seconds of arc." A degree contains 60 minutes of arc and a minute contains 60 seconds of arc. For example, the US capitol is located at 38°53'23"N , 77°00'27"W (38 degrees, 53 minutes, and 23 seconds north of the equator and 77 degrees, no minutes, and 27 seconds west of the meridian passing through Greenwich, England).

Finally, to precisely identify a location on, in, or above the earth, one has to also specify the elevation or altitude above the earth's surface, or above a fixed frame of reference like sea level. Using the three measurements of longitude, latitude, and altitude, the "mile high" city of Denver, Colorado, would be at 39 degrees, 45 minutes, and 3 seconds north latitude (39°45'3"N), and 104 degrees, 54 minutes, and 35 seconds west longitude (104°54'35"W.) Denver's altitude, measured on the fifteenth step of the state capitol building is 5,280 feet (one mile, or 1.6 km) high.

Geodesists are scientists who work to determine the exact position of geographical points. They study the size, shape and gravitational field of the earth. They use surveying and geodetic instruments, such as transits and theodolites, to set up and improve networks of triangulation over the earth's surface. These altitude and location "benchmarks" provide fixed points for use in making maps. With the natural shifts in our environment (from plate movements, erosion, wind, urbanization, etc.), the exact location of many places can change frequently, making geodetic work very important. New technologies including aerial photography, satellite imagery, and geopositioning devices are being used to improve the accuracy of maps.

76. What are the four major directions? In which direction does the needle of a compass point?

The four major directions are north, south, east, and west; a compass needle points north.

A compass, often used when hiking or sailing, is a navigational tool used to tell direction. Magnets in the compass align themselves along a magnetic north-south orientation, which causes the needle to align with the magnetic North Pole, so it points north. The compass card inside the glass has the four headings shown as N, E, S, and W (going clockwise) and subheadings of northeast, southeast, southwest, and northwest. Numbers appear every 30 degrees. Long vertical marks occur every 10 degrees, with intervening short marks at 5-degree points. The compass card containing the magnets is mounted on a small pivot point in the center of the card assembly. This allows the compass card to rotate and float freely. The enclosure of the compass is filled with white kerosene to provide a medium to dampen out vibrations and unwanted oscillations. A lubber line is etched onto the glass face of the instrument to enable exact reading of the compass.

When a compass points north, it is pointing towards magnetic north, or in the direction of the earth's magnetic field. True north, also known as geographical north, is the actual northernmost point on the earth, or the center of the North Pole. The two measurements differ because the Earth's magnetic "north pole" is actually in Canada. In order for an explorer to determine his actual location, he has to know the difference between true north and magnetic north, which changes depending on the longitude.

77. What is the earth's circumference?

The earth's circumference is 24,902 miles (40,075 km). The polar circumference of the earth is 24,860 miles (40,008 km).

The first fairly accurate estimate of the earth's circumference was made by a Greek named Eratosthenes around 200 BC. His estimate was about 28,750 miles (46,268 km), and was based on variations of the sun's position in the sky on June 21st in two different locations. Greeks and Egyptians were the first to use latitude and longitude and to share the concept of measuring the earth's circumference.

The English word "equator" comes from the fourteenth century Latin word *aequator*, meaning equalizer. The equator passes through thirteen countries: Ecuador, Colombia, Brazil, Sao Tomé and Principe, Gabon, Republic of the Congo, Uganda, Kenya, Somalia, Republic of Maldives, Indonesia, and Kiribati. (In Maldives and Kiribati, the equator passes within territorial sea, 12 nautical miles, but does not touch land.) The "Village of Equator" in Western Kenya is on the western rim of the Great Rift Valley and, of course, on the equator.

78. Which place has no land, only ice: the North Pole or the South Pole?

The North Pole.

There is no land at the North Pole, the northern end of the earth's axis. Located at 90 degrees north latitude, the North Pole is covered by sea ice. Sea ice is formed from ocean water that freezes. Because the oceans are salty, this occurs at about 30.2°F (-1.8°C). Pack ice is floating, consolidated sea ice that's detached and freely floating, not attached to land. Wider chunks of ice are called ice fields.

At the South Pole, Antarctica, on the tops of some of the mountains there are areas without ice or snow, and along the coast there are also areas with no ice, or snow. Much of the South Pole was formed from volcanic activity. At the South Pole, a scientific station named McMurdo has ice and snow on parts of it, but much of this station is on volcanic rock and dirt. Another part of Antarctica, called Dry Valleys, has no snow or ice. Antarctica is the coldest, windiest, and driest continent on the planet. It receives almost no precipitation of any kind. Since a desert is defined as somewhere that receives less than ten inches of precipitation per year, Antarctica is technically a desert!

79. The continental divide separates:
    a) which animals are nocturnal and which are diurnal.
    b) the Northern Hemisphere from the Southern Hemisphere.
    c) the direction water travels to the sea.
    d) where it rains from where it snows.

    The North American continental divide is a mountain ridge that runs irregularly north and south through the Rocky Mountains and separates eastward-flowing from westward-flowing waterways. The waters that flow eastward empty into the Gulf of Mexico by way of the Mississippi and other rivers. The waters that flow westward empty into the Pacific Ocean.

    Every continent with the exception of Antarctica has a continental divide. Some continents may have more than one. North America also has an eastern continental divide, which runs along the Appalachian Mountains. Rivers to the west of this divide drain into the Mississippi and other rivers that flow into the Gulf of Mexico. Waterways to the east of the divide flow into the Atlantic Ocean.

    Nocturnal and diurnal refers to the active time for an organism. An animal that is active during the day and rests at night is diurnal. An animal that primarily rests during the day and is active at night is nocturnal.

    The equator, an imaginary line drawn around the earth halfway between the north and south poles, separates the northern and southern hemispheres. (See question 77.)

Rain is liquid precipitation while snow is solid crystals. There are several factors that affect whether precipitation falls as snow or rain, such as temperature and elevation. (See question 87.)

80. What covers the majority of the earth's surface?
a) oceans   c) desert
b) glaciers   d) grasslands

Although ice (in the form of glaciers and tundra), desert, and rocks combine with other features such as mountains, lakes, rivers, and grasslands to form part of the earth's surface, oceans cover the most—approximately 71 percent of the earth's surface.

The Pacific Ocean covers the largest area and is also the world's deepest ocean. Sir Arthur C. Clarke (British author and inventor, most famous for his science-fiction novel *2001: A Space Odyssey*) once said, "How inappropriate to call this planet Earth, when it clearly is Ocean." This ocean presence, coupled with how water reflects and scatters light, is why Earth is so often referred to as "the blue planet."

Glaciers are large bodies of ice moving slowly down a slope or spreading across a land surface. (See question 78.)

Deserts are dry places that typically average less than ten inches (25 cm) of precipitation per year. Plants in the desert tend to lose water quickly through evaporation.

Grasslands are large areas filled with grasses, flowers, and other low-growing plants.

81. Most of the fresh water on this planet is stored in:
   (a) the Great Lakes.
   (b) the many rivers and streams on the earth.
   (c) reservoirs built by humans.
☞ **(d) polar ice caps.**

The polar ice caps contain more fresh water than all the Great Lakes together. (The polar ice caps cover the North and South Pole regions.) Antarctic ice alone represents about nearly two-thirds of the world's fresh water. The volume of all the polar ice caps (both north and south) is very important, because it may provide answers to future problems regarding the earth's fresh water supply.

The Great Lakes are large, containing 6 quadrillion gallons of fresh water, which is 95 percent of the freshwater in the US. They make up one-fifth of the world's fresh surface water, second only to the polar ice caps and Lake Baikal in Siberia. Spread evenly across the continental US., the Great Lakes would submerge the country under about 9.5 feet (2.9 m) of water.

Rivers and streams are where we get much of our drinking water, but these make up only a tiny fraction of the world's fresh water supply. Man-made reservoirs make up even less.

Other water sources involve collecting rainwater and tapping groundwater through wells. This water supply, however, is not adequate for human consumption, and water purification is needed. Popular methods for purifying water are filtering, boiling, and distillation. Governments in many countries have programs to distribute water to the needy at no charge. Reducing waste, or using drinking water only for human consumption, is another way to keep supplies under control. In some cities, such as Hong Kong, sea water is used for flushing toilets citywide in order to conserve fresh water resources. (See question 24 and the earth science bonus question.)

82. The day with the most hours of sunlight occurs in what month in the Northern Hemisphere? In the Southern Hemisphere?

Northern Hemisphere: June
Southern Hemisphere: December

The longest day of the year in the Northern Hemisphere is on or around June 21st, and is known as the summer solstice. In the Northern Hemisphere, the longest day of the year is when the overhead position of the sun is farthest north. The length of time elapsed between sunrise and sunset on this day is the maximum for the whole year. The summer solstice marks the first day of the season of summer. In the Southern Hemisphere, winter and summer solstices are opposite those in the Northern Hemisphere. Because of this, the longest day of the year in the Southern Hemisphere will be around December 21st. This is the summer solstice for the Southern Hemisphere.

83. In the spring and fall, the hours of daylight and darkness are the same on what two days?

The equinoxes, on or near March 21st and September 21st.

Day and night are nearly of equal length at the time of the March and September equinoxes. The dates on which day and night are each twelve hours are actually a few days before and after the equinoxes. The specific dates of this occurrence are different for different latitudes. On the day of an equinox, the geometric center of the sun's disk crosses the equator, and this point is above the horizon for twelve hours everywhere on Earth. However, the sun is not simply a geometric point. Sunrise is defined as the instant when the leading edge of the sun's disk becomes visible on the horizon, whereas sunset is the instant when the trailing edge of the disk disappears below the horizon. These are the moments of first and last direct sunlight.

84. Why is it colder an hour after sunrise than it is at sunrise itself?

Because the planet continues losing heat after sunrise.

We think the minimum temperature should occur at sunrise because the earth has been cooling down all night. The temperature drops throughout the night because of two processes. The earth no longer receives energy from the sun and the earth radiates energy to space. Overnight, the balance is strongly negative and the earth loses heat.

At sunrise, solar energy again arrives, but the heat loss due to radiation to space dominates until about an hour after sunrise. At that time, incoming solar radiation increases enough to overcome the radiational heat loss.

85. In a weather forecast, what is the difference between a *watch* and a *warning*?

A watch is for something potential; a warning is for verified or imminent conditions.

A weather watch is issued by the National Weather Service and indicates that a particular hazard is possible, meaning that conditions are more favorable than usual for its occurrence. A watch is a time for preparing, paying attention to weather information, and thinking about what to do if the danger materializes.

A weather warning issued by the weather service indicates that a particular weather hazard is either imminent or is reported to be taking place. A warning indicates the need to take action to protect life and property, and to move out of harm's way as soon as possible. The type of warning defines the hazard and recommended safety (a tornado warning, blizzard warning, hurricane warning, etc.).

86. During a thunderstorm, does lightning appear before or after you hear thunder?

Lightning appears before you hear thunder.

You see lightning first because light travels faster than sound. But it is also the lightning that creates the thunder.

Lightning is actually a gigantic spark. The spark is created because giant separations between a positive and negative charge develop within a thunderstorm cloud, between one cloud and another, and between the cloud and the ground. As raindrops, hailstones, and snowflakes pass by each other, electrical charge separations develop. It's much like rubbing a balloon on a wool sweater. Motions within the cloud move the charged precipitation around, creating some places where negative charges dominate and others where this less negative (i.e., positive) charge prevails. When the difference between positive and negative is so large that the air cannot insulate it anymore, a discharge or spark, known as lightning, can occur.

Once lightning happens, the air inside the lightning channel can be heated to as much as 50,000°F (27,760°C), 4.5 times the surface temperature of the sun. As the heated air expands, it bumps into the air outside the channel. The result is a giant sound wave that moves away from the lightning flash, otherwise known as thunder.

Since lightning travels at 186,000 miles (299,338 km) per second (the speed of light) and thunder travels at only about 1,040 feet (317 m) per second (the speed of sound), we see lightning first.

During a storm, if you want to know how far away you are from the lightning, simply count (using one-one thousand, two-one thousand, three-one thousand, etc.) from the time you see the lightning until you hear the thunder. For each "one-one thousand" you count, the lightning is 0.2 miles (0.3 km) away. For example, if you counted to three-one thousand, the lightning is three times 0.2 miles (0.3 km), or 0.6 miles (1 km) away. If there is almost no time between the lightning and the thunder, the lightning is too close for comfort!

87. Name three kinds of precipitation.

Rain, drizzle, hail, freezing rain, sleet, and snow are all different kinds of precipitation.

When the precipitation becomes too heavy to remain suspended in the air inside of clouds, it falls to the ground. Precipitation occurs in a variety of forms—some frozen, some liquid.

Rain develops when growing cloud droplets become too heavy to remain in the cloud and, as a result, fall toward the surface of the earth. The raindrops start out as drizzle, which can float to the earth as well, but slowly. However, as the drizzle-sized drops bump into other drops, they attach and grow larger, making true raindrops.

If the rain falls into a colder layer on its way down, the raindrops can freeze into small balls of ice known as sleet. If the rain falls on trees, roads, or cars whose temperature is below freezing, the water may freeze on impact. This is known as freezing rain, or glaze.

Hail is a large frozen raindrop produced by intense thunderstorms, where snow and rain can co-exist in a central updraft in the storm. This updraft can carry raindrops upwards into the colder, upper portions of the cloud where the rain freezes. If the updraft is strong enough, it can keep the hailstone suspended, allowing it to either take a series of up-and-down trips (where it can collect a watery skin and then freeze), or the hailstone can be kept in the cold portion of the storm as supercooled water (water as low as -40°F or -40°C) collects on it. Once the hailstone becomes too heavy to be supported by the updraft, it falls from the sky. The hailstone can reach the ground as ice since it is not in the warm air below the storm long enough to melt completely. If a hailstone the size of a golf ball reaches the ground, think how big it must have been inside the cloud!

Snowflakes are simply a combination of ice crystals that collect and stick to each other as they fall toward the surface of the earth from the clouds above. Since the snowflakes do not pass through a layer of air warm enough to cause them to melt, they remain intact and reach the ground as snow.

88. What elements must be present for a rainbow to appear?

Light and precipitation.

When precipitation is falling on the side of the sky away from the sun, and the sun is relatively low in the sky behind you, the sun can shine where the precipitation is falling. As the sunlight strikes the falling raindrops, some light enters the drops and is bent (refracted). Since light is composed of all colors and the amount of refraction depends on the wavelength of the light (violets have short wavelengths and reds longer ones), each color experiences a different amount of bending. Then the separated colors reflect off the inner-back surface of the raindrop, and finally, they pass through the raindrop again, returning toward you. If the angle between the sun, the falling rain, and your eyes is around 40°, you may see a bow. Red will be on the outside of the bow and the blues and violets on the inside. Sometimes light will experience more than one internal reflection inside the raindrops. When this happens, you may see a double rainbow, with the colors reversed.

We cannot follow the arc of a rainbow down below the horizon, because we cannot see water droplets in the air below the horizon. But the higher we are above the ground, the more of the rainbow circle we see. That is why from an airplane in flight a rainbow can appear as a complete circle with the shadow of the airplane in the center.

You can sometimes also see rainbows in the spray from waterfalls, hoses, and fountains. (For more on reflection, see question 68.)

89. What is the difference between a hurricane and a tornado?

A tornado is small and generally forms over land; a hurricane forms over warm oceans.

A hurricane is a tropical storm in which winds reach speeds of at least 74 miles (119 km) per hour. Hurricanes start over the ocean as a collection of thunderstorms in tropical areas. Sometimes the thunderstorms can actually form over Africa and move over warm Atlantic waters. Under certain conditions, winds can start to spin around the cloud area and a tropical depression can form. As winds increase, the depression can grow into a tropical storm (and be given a name), and possibly a hurricane.

Once a tropical storm becomes a hurricane, it often has an eye, a relatively calm center region that has fewer clouds (sometimes it's almost cloud-free) with little, if any, precipitation. You can see this eye in weather satellite and weather radar images.

Hurricanes come in many different sizes and shapes. Some are small enough to fit inside New Jersey. Others, like Katrina and Rita in 2005, can fill up a large part of the Gulf of Mexico. Some hurricanes can remain weak, with winds of 74-95 miles (119-153 km) per hour. Others can become very intense, with sustained winds of 155 miles (249 km) per hour or more.

The greatest danger from hurricanes is not wind, but water. Storm surge (the push of water onto a coastal area) and flooding from heavy rainfall cause the greatest destruction and loss of life.

90. What type of scale do seismologists use to measure the strength of an earthquake?

Richter scale.

For almost three-quarters of a century, seismologists, or scientists who study earthquakes and seismic waves, have used the Richter scale to measure an earthquake's strength or magnitude. Dr. Charles Richter developed the scale in 1935 when he recognized that the seismic waves radiated by all earthquakes can provide good estimates of their magnitudes. The earthquake itself occurs when adjacent rock layers suddenly slip and slide along each other.

The Richter scale provides a calibrated magnitude rating of seismic waves and their resulting earthquakes, ranging from less than 2 (not felt by humans) to 8 or greater (capable of causing mass destruction). Scientists measure these waves using seismographs, which record a zigzag trace on a seismogram showing the varying degree of ground motions beneath its sensor. Sensitive seismographs placed in strategic locations around the planet can now register earthquakes of 4.5 or higher anywhere in the world. Annually, there are eighteen major earthquakes (7 or higher) around the world; compare this to some 1.4 million combined minor and very minor earthquakes (3.9 or less).

Because the magnitude scale is based on powers of 10, an earthquake with a magnitude of 6.5 has ten times the wave amplitude (or height) on a seismogram. This relates to a 6.5 earthquake having about 30 times the energy of a 5.3 earthquake. Earthquake damage is not entirely dependent on the strength of the quake; building codes of that area, population density, underlying ground structures, and the distance of places from the earthquake itself also have an effect.

General Science Answers

91. What does the suffix "ology" mean?

"ology" means a field of study or branch of science.

From its Greek root, "ology" means "the study of." We get a specific branch of study when we add a prefix to this suffix, or word ending. For example, the prefix "bio" means life, or living organism. Biology, then, means the study of living things. "Geo" means earth; geology is the study of the earth. Volcanology is the study of volcanoes. The suffix "onomy" is nearly the same as "ology" and means "the science of." Astronomy is the science of the universe; taxonomy is the science of classifying of living organisms.

92. What is a hypothesis?

A proposed explanation for why something happens.

In common usage today, a hypothesis (which is Greek for assumption) is a provisional idea whose merit must be evaluated. Science happens in many ways. In some instances, a scientist observes a phenomenon—such as, food left at room temperature spoils more rapidly than food kept cool—and then develops a hypothesis for why. Other times, scientists set out to answer a question—such as, will mice be healthier if they eat vegetables or chocolate. Whether the hypothesis comes from an intellectual pursuit or an observation, the job of scientists is to perform tests in order to validate or negate their ideas. Through rigorous testing, scientists can help us learn what is speculation and what is real.

93. What are the two most common measurements of temperature?

Fahrenheit and Celsius.

Temperature is the measure of the warmth or coolness of an object. It is measured with a thermometer or another instrument that has a scale calibrated in degrees. The size of a degree depends on the particular temperature scale being used. A temperature scale is determined by choosing two reference temperatures and dividing the temperature difference between these two points into a certain number of degrees. The two reference temperatures used for most common scales are the melting point of ice and the boiling point of water. On the Celsius temperature scale, also referred to as the Centigrade scale, the melting point of ice is set at 0°C, the boiling point of pure water (at sea level) is set at 100°C, and the difference between them is divided into 100 degrees. On the Fahrenheit temperature scale, the melting point is set at 32°F, the boiling point at 212°F, and the difference between them is equal to 180 degrees.

Temperatures on the Fahrenheit scale can be converted to equivalent temperatures on the Celsius scale by first subtracting 32 from the Fahrenheit temperature, then multiplying the result by 5/9, according to the formula $(F-32) \times 5/9 = C$. So, 59°F is the same as 15°C.

Although the Fahrenheit scale was formerly used widely in English-speaking countries, many of these countries began changing to the more convenient Celsius temperature scale in the late 1960s and early 1970s; a notable exception is the United States, where the Fahrenheit scale is still in common use, along with other English units of measurement.

94. How many pounds does one cup of water weigh?

Half a pound.

There are two primary types of measurement systems, English units and metric units. The United States is one of the few countries in the world that still uses the English unit measuring system. The English system measures in pounds (lb), gallons (gal), pints (pt), yards (yd), feet (ft), inches (in), and miles (mi); while the metric system measures in liters (l), kilometers (km), meters (m), grams (g), etc. For liquid measure, or liquid capacity, the basic English unit is the gallon, which is divided into 4 quarts, 8 pints, or 32 gills. There are 2 cups in a pint and therefore, 16 cups in a gallon. One gallon of liquid weighs approximately 8 pounds. Therefore 1 cup of liquid would weigh 0.5 pounds. A handy method to remember this is the phrase, "a pint's a pound the world around."

95. Which weighs more: a ton of apples or a ton of feathers?

They weigh the same amount.

First, what is a ton? Regardless of what you're weighing, a net ton is a unit of weight measurement that equals 2,000 pounds, or 907.18 kilograms. The British term gross ton (t) is 2,240 pounds, and a metric ton (mt) equals 1,000 kilograms or 2,204.6 pounds. Regardless of which ton you're using, a ton of apples and a ton of feathers weigh the same . . . a ton! However, since feathers are so much lighter than apples, it would take a much greater volume of them to make up a ton.

96. When scientists are performing an experiment, they make changes to the conditions that brought about a particular phenomenon to see how those changes affect what they are studying. How many things do scientists change at a time?

One.

When a scientist is investigating a phenomenon, two things are very important: recording each result as accurately as possible and maintaining appropriate laboratory conditions. A scientist must carefully document what happens when each new activity or item is brought into the experiment. For example, if she is trying to discover the effect that light has on a plant, she will introduce the same amount of light and the same kind of light each time she exposes the plant to light. The soil, moisture, type of container, etc., must all be kept as similar as possible because a change in any one of these could affect the plant, too. When she tests a new scenario, she must only change one variable at a time, such as the duration of light, the intensity of light, or the color of light. Laboratory equipment is highly specialized to aid in experiments and to help the scientist create reliable, uncontaminated conditions for their experiments.

However, not all science experiments lend themselves to single changes. Sometimes scientists cannot control all the variables; in these cases, repeating the experiment multiple times helps reduce the effect of random error.

97. Why do scientists wear white lab coats?

To protect themselves and their clothing.

On the whole, scientists do not wear white clothes. They wear much the same sort of clothes as anyone else. But when they are handling potentially dangerous substances in the laboratory, they put on safety glasses to protect their eyes, and a longish white cotton jacket (a laboratory coat) to protect their clothes and themselves in the event of a spill. They also usually wear cuffless trousers and shoes with closed tops. Why are lab coats white? Partly it is to make contamination as visible as possible, but it is also just tradition. While a lab coat does not offer complete protection for a fire or explosion or major spill, it is an extra layer of clothing which can be quickly removed along with most of the hazardous material. It does stop minor splashes of poisonous or corrosive materials. A lab coat should be kept in a special locker or rack at the workplace (preferably right at the laboratory entrance), and cleaned regularly.

98. What is a control group?

A group relative to which observers can measure change.

In many science experiments, the goal is to determine the effect of a certain factor on a certain population. For example, a scientist might want to test whether a new medication can help people with learning disabilities focus better in class. The scientist would give the medicine to a group of people and then, through surveys and tests, determine whether it was effective.

However, people tend to believe that taking medicine will help them feel better or perform better. This could influence the study negatively, because the group being tested could imagine results that aren't actually there. To try to make up for this, a control group is used. This group would be given a placebo, which wouldn't have any medicine in it, just sugar or other inactive ingredients. This group would also experience any imagined effects from the idea of taking a pill, and so hopefully, when their results were compared to the experiment group, the real results would be seen.

99. What is the goal of a double-blind, placebo-controlled study?

To eliminate the chance of bias.

In a single-blind experiment, the individual subjects do not know whether they are so-called test subjects or members of an experimental control group, but the researchers do. In such an experiment, there is a risk that the subjects are influenced by interaction with the researchers. This is known as the experimenter effect.

Double-blind describes an especially stringent way of conducting a scientific experiment. In a double-blind experiment, neither the individuals nor the scientists know who belongs to the control group. Only after all the data is recorded (and in some cases, analyzed) are scientists permitted to learn which individuals are which. Performing an experiment in double-blind fashion is a way to lessen the influence of prejudice and unintentional cues on the results. Strictly speaking, in this type of experiment, every scientist who interacts with or treats a subject should be "blinded." This doesn't mean that they are really sight-impaired, it means they don't know who is receiving a particular test or intervention.

100. Name some important motives for studying science.

Curiosity, finding a solution to a problem, fame, wealth, and a desire to help the planet and its inhabitants.

Curiosity and intelligence are examples of having an interest in something and experimenting to see what would happen or what can happen by creating specific effects. Scientists often use a systematic process of inquiry in order to discover or revise facts, events, behaviors, or theories.

Sometimes a researcher wants to find a solution to a problem. Garrett A. Morgan invented a traffic signal. In 1914, his traffic signal system, the first of its kind, was installed in Cleveland, Ohio. This scientific invention was started in response to the growing problems of pedestrian safety after the invention of the automobile.

Albert Einstein is a household name and among the most famous scientists, but he never became wealthy during his life in the United States. Born in 1879 into a wealthy family in Germany, he emigrated to America after the Nazi government confiscated his property and revoked his citizenship. Einstein joined the Institute for Advanced Study in Princeton, New Jersey, where he remained until his death in 1955. (See question 50.)

Sometimes people are very rich, but not famous. Though his wealth is certainly no secret, the world's fourth-richest person (at press time) remains a well-kept secret. Paul Allen made his fortune as Bill Gates's partner, developing computers for personal use, and helping to make Microsoft an enormously successful company. He has been dubbed the accidental zillionaire.

Dr. Jonas Salk, who discovered the polio vaccine, helped people around the globe through medical discovery. In 1947,

Dr. Salk became the director of the virus research lab at the University of Pittsburgh. While working on improving the flu vaccine, he began to study poliovirus in hopes of creating a vaccine against that debilitating disease. In 1952, he first inoculated volunteers—including himself, his wife, and their three sons—with a polio vaccine made from the killed virus.

Scientific research is very often conducted when a scientist has an interest in helping someone. Alexander Graham Bell, who studied acoustics and created the telephone, was also committed to applying his work to help or cure his mother, who was deaf. He pioneered lip reading in an attempt at utilizing the acute sight of many deaf people. Educated at the Royal High School of Edinburgh (Scotland), he graduated at the age of 13.

101. In ancient Greece, what were scientists called?

Philosophers.

In ancient Greece, the study of the natural world was very closely connected to the search for truth about existence in general. They believed in a direct relationship, between physical elements and human behavior, which led to the connection between the fields of philosophy and science (which did not yet exist in the defined form it does now). In modern times, we refer to these Greeks as both scientists and philosophers.

Socrates was one of the most famous philosophers of his time. He lived and studied in Athens in the fifth century BC. Due to his strong commitment to truth, he displayed a great deal of interest in scientific theories about the physical world. Anaximander was also a Greek philosopher who lived about one hundred years before Socrates. He believed that all matter resulted from the distillation of hot, cold, dry, and wet elements from *apeirwn*, which in Greek means the boundless extent of the universe. Examination of fossils persuaded Anaximander that living beings developed from simple to more complex over time.

In modern times, the fields of philosophy and science have separated, but questions about the physical world and the world of philosophical inquiry are still seen by many to be connected at the root.

Bonus
Answers

Biology

What percentage of all mammals are carnivores?

Six percent.

A true carnivore is an animal that subsists primarily on a diet of flesh. There are approximately 4,200 known species of mammals, of which about 250 are meat-eaters. That puts carnivores at about 6 percent of the total number of mammals. Of course, many of these species do not exclusively eat meat—many also eat plant foods and honey. Some examples of carnivores are polar bears, lions, foxes, and walruses.

Even though carnivores are flesh-eaters by definition, there are some whose diets are made up of just as much plant matter as flesh. The giant panda, for example, is categorized as a carnivore, but it also eats a lot of bamboo shoots. What an animal eats also has a lot to do with what is available. For instance, there are several species, like mice and rats, that are categorized as herbivores but will eat meat in some situations.

Since carnivores are meat-eaters, they must have claws, teeth, or sharp beaks to tear into their food. They also have eyes which face forward, helping them judge the distance to their prey when they are hunting.

Herbivores are animals whose diets consist mostly of plants. They have flat teeth suited to chewing tough plant material, feet made for running, and eyes that point towards the side. A good way to remember the difference between carnivores and hebivores is this rhyme: Eyes to the front, likes to hunt. Eyes to the side, likes to hide.

Physics

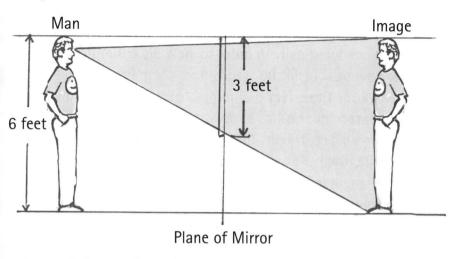

Man   Image

3 feet

6 feet

Plane of Mirror

How tall does a flat mirror have to be for you to be able to see your entire image reflected in it?

Half your size.

A mirror has a very smooth, flat, shiny surface capable of reflecting sufficient undiffused light to form an image of an object placed in front of it. Often, the main reflecting surface in a mirror is a metallic backing that reflects light, instead of absorbing it like a nonreflective surface does. The metallic surface is much more reflective than glass, which allows most of the light to pass through. (You can sometimes see reflections on smooth polished furniture and on smooth lakes, as well.) A flat mirror with a good metallic backing can reflect a near-perfect image. We use mirrors in a variety of ways every day. Drivers use them to see the cars around them, dentists use them to inspect our teeth, and scientists use them in microscopes and telescopes to reflect images.

To view your full image in a flat or "plane" mirror, you will need a mirror equal to half your height. In other words, a man six feet (1.8 m) tall needs a mirror that is three feet (0.9 m) tall positioned vertically in order to view his entire image. No matter how near or far he stands from the mirror, he still needs a mirror three feet (0.9m) high to see his entire image.

The reason for this has to do with the angle the light hits the mirror surface. If light hit a mirror not quite head on, but at an angle, then the reflected light would leave the surface at the same angle in relation to a line drawn normal (or perpendicular) to the surface of the mirror. The angle that the

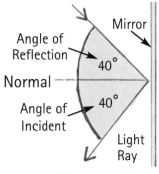

light hits the surface of the mirror is measured from the normal and is called the angle of incidence. The angle that the light bounces off the surface of the mirror is the same angle measured from the normal, at the opposite side, and is known as the angle of reflection. Thus, the angle of incidence equals the angle of reflection.

When you look at your image in a mirror, you look from your eyes up to the top of your head and from your eyes down to your feet. Since the angle of incidence is the same as the angle of reflection, you only need to look halfway to your feet to be able to see them reflected in the mirror. The same goes for looking up at the top of your head.

You can try this yourself and even prove that it doesn't matter how far away from the mirror you stand. Stand about three feet (0.9m) away from the mirror and have a friend, using soap, mark where you see your toes and where the top of your head is in the mirror. Measure your height and the distance between the soap marks. Now take two steps away from the mirror and repeat. You can see that you only need a mirror equal to half your height to see your whole body.

Chemistry

What metal is a liquid at room temperature?

Mercury.

Mercury is the only metal that is a liquid at room temperature, although francium, cesium, gallium and rubidium are all metals that melt just a few degrees above room temperature. The bonds between mercury atoms are very weak and are easily overcome by heat, so it boils and melts at lower temperatures than any other metal. Although mercury is a liquid, it is not wet. Its surface tension is different than other liquids, so it does not soak into material, but runs right off instead. Mercury rarely occurs freely in nature and is found mainly in cinnabar ore (HgS) in Spain and Italy.

Mercury was used in equipment like thermometers, barometers, and mirrors, but it is a neurotoxin; as a matter of fact the term "mad as a hatter" came about because mercury was used in making hats. It was applied to hats to make the felt lie flat and give it a high gloss. The mercury would slowly seep through the skull of the wearer and cause madness.

Most household fever thermometers no longer use mercury, but if you do have one and it breaks, extreme care must be taken in cleaning up and disposing of the spilled mercury so that it does not touch your skin or spread to other surfaces in your house. Even mercury vapor at room temperature has enough vapor pressure to be absorbed by breathing. If you add sulfur to spilled mercury, a chemical reaction will occur, producing a black, hard substance. This can be sucked up using a special vacuum cleaner and disposed of. However, should you spill mercury, you should call your state pollution control office for disposal instructions. (See question 39.)

Earth Science

Throughout history, people have fought wars over natural resources such as salt, land, and oil. Scientists are concerned that another resource will be the reason for the next global conflict. What resource is it?

Water.

Water is essential to all forms of life. Fresh water has become scarce because of the world's growing population, increased contamination through pollution, and global warming. While the amount of salt water on the planet is enormous, continuing availability of clean, fresh water is a major social and economic concern.

Water is a strategic resource for many countries. Many battles and wars have been fought to gain access to it. UNESCO (United Nation's Educational, Scientific, and Cultural Organization) has a World Water Development Program which predicts that in the next twenty years the quantity of fresh water available to everyone will decrease, leaving one-third of the world's inhabitants without enough fresh water for minimal hygiene. Already there have been many situations in which the lack of safe drinking-water supplies have affected large populations. For example, in 2000, more than 2.2 million people died from diseases related to the consumption of contaminated water or drought. In 2004, the British charitable organization WaterAid reported that a child dies every fifteen seconds due to easily preventable water-related diseases. Some have predicted that clean water will become the next oil, making Canada, with this resource in abundance, possibly the richest country in the world. (See questions 24 and 81.)

General Science

What is the source of all energy on Earth?

The sun.

The energy source for all life on our planet is the sun. The sun, the closest star to Earth, is a huge ball of molten (glowing) gas that provides energy in many ways.

The most obvious are light and heat, which keep us warm. The sun also provides energy that allows green plants to grow. Green plants use the sun's energy to split water into hydrogen and oxygen through a process known as photosynthesis, the ultimate source of all food on Earth. By using the sun's energy this way, green plants give animals the food they need to survive. Animals eat plants and other animals, in turn, eat the plant-eaters. When an animal or plant dies, its energy goes back into the earth, converting from flesh and plant material back into soil with the help of special microbes that continue the never-ending energy cycle.

Additionally, solar energy, including radio waves, x-rays, and light, can also be used to power our cars and homes. Fossil fuels, such as gasoline and coal are derived from animals and small plants that were dependent on the sun's energy millions of years ago. Hydroelectrical energy and even wind energy are made possible by the sun. The sun evaporates water from the oceans, lakes, and rivers, and this water vapor forms clouds. The rain falls back to the ground and flows in rivers. We build dams to harness that energy and use it as electricity. Wind energy also comes from the sun's power. Because the sun heats our planet unevenly, air flows from colder to warmer areas, creating wind. (See questions 57 and 71.)

Science Resources

Organizations

American Association for the Advancement of Science (www.aaas.org)

An international non-profit organization serving as an educator, professional association, and a leader. The association publishes newsletters and journals all dedicated to fulfilling the mission of advancing science and helping society.

Contact Information:
AAAS
1200 New York Avenue NW
Washington, DC 20005
Tel: (202) 326-6400
webmaster@aaas.org

Links for parents and teachers:

http://www.aaas.org/port_educators.shtml
This link provides additional sources, newsletters, and information for teachers.
http://www.aaas.org/port_kid.shtml
This link provides additional information on how parents can get involved and help promote the love of learning for their child/children.

Carnegie Academy for the Advancement of Science

(http://carnegieinstitution.org/first_light_case/about_case.html)
The CASE program is an educational resource, designed to increase Washington, DC public school teachers' knowledge of science. The program introduces new methods of teaching to bring science to students.

Contact Information:
Carnegie Academy for Science Education
1530 P Street, N.W. Washington, D.C. 20005
Tel: (202) 939-1135
Fax: (202) 387-8092 Fax
case@pst.ciw.edu

Links for parents and teachers:

http://carnegieinstitution.org/first_light_case/Curriculum.htm
This link for teachers introduces instruction plans by grade.
http://carnegieinstitution.org/first_light_case/other_links_1.htm
This link allows teachers to retrieve more information and additional resources related to science and teaching.

Centers for Disease Control (www.cdc.gov)

The Centers for Disease Control is part of the Department of Health and Human Services. Founded in 1946 to assist in controlling malaria, CDC is still "at the forefront of public health efforts to prevent and control infectious and chronic diseases." They also help reduce workplace hazards and environmental health issues. Globally recognized, CDC attempts to apply its research to improving people's lives and responding to any emergencies that may arise.

Contact Information:
Centers for Disease Control and Prevention
Public Inquiries/MASO
Mailstop F07
1600 Clifton Road
Atlanta, GA 30333
Tel: (800) 311-3435

Environmental Protection Agency (http://www.epa.gov/)

The Environmental Protection Agency aims to protect human health and the environment. EPA leads the nation's environmental science, research, and education.

Contact Information:
Environmental Protection Agency
Ariel Rios Building
1200 Pennsylvania Avenue, NW
Washington, DC 20460
Tel: (202) 272-0167

Links for parents and teachers:

http://www.epa.gov/teachers/
This link offers background information on a variety of topics, lesson plans, and activities for both in the classroom and outside the classroom.
http://www.epa.gov/epahome/educational.htm
This link provides information that targets kids with games and projects relating to the environment, and provides older children with concepts and activities and high school students with a very informative resource center.

National Aeronautics and Space Administration

(http://www.gsfc.nasa.gov/science.html)
NASA's website offers a science question of the week, a perfect way to keep expanding science knowledge. They also offer games and activities online for children, educational resources for students, and an interactive program that simulates a NASA mission.

Contact Information:
NASA Headquarters
300 E St. SW
Washington, D.C. 20024
Tel: (202) 358-0000
Fax: (202) 358-3251

National Association of Biology Teachers (www.nabt.org)

NABT is an organization which encompasses the leaders of life science education. The website allows educators the opportunity to share their experiences and expertise with other colleagues from around the country.

Contact Information:
NABT
12030 Sunrise Valley Drive, Suite 110,
Reston VA 20191
Voice: (703) 264-9696, (800) 406-0775
office@nabt.org

National Biological Information Infrastructure (NBII)

(http://www.nbii.gov/index.html)
The National Biological Information Infrastructure is a collaborative program which provides information on the nation's biological resources.

Contact Information:
USGS Biological Informatics Office
302 National Center
Reston, Virginia 20192
Tel: (703) 648-NBII (6244)
Fax: (703) 648-4224

Links for parents and teachers:

http://www.nbii.gov/education/index.html
This link provides many resources for parents and teachers. The site is organized by subject (General Curriculum, Aquatic Biology, Birds, Botany, and Mammals, etc). Within each subject are a variety of activities and information for students of all ages (grades K-12).

National Education Association (http://www.nea.org/index.html)

The National Education Association is devoted to advancing the cause of public education.

Contact Information:
1201 16th Street, NW
Washington, DC 20036-3290
Tel: (202) 833-4000 (Monday-Friday 8:30 a.m. - 4:30 p.m. ET)
Fax: (202) 822-7974

Links for parents and teachers:

http://www.nea.org/member/index.html
This link provides additional articles for educators and also offers lesson plan ideas, information on classroom management, and further research relating to teaching.
http://www.nea.org/parents/index.html
This link offers an index of more links for parents. Links contain research and guides for parents to get more involved with their children's education.

National Oceanic and Atmospheric Administration (http://www.noaa.gov/)

The National Oceanic and Atmospheric Administration's mission statement is "to understand and predict changes in the earth's environment and conserve and manage coastal and marine resources to meet our nation's economic, social, and environmental needs." Their website contains links to information about things such as weather, oceans, climate, and fisheries.

Contact Information:
14th Street Constitution Avenue, NW
Room 6217
Washington, DC 20230
Tel: (202) 482-6090
Fax: (202) 482-3154

National Science Foundation (www.nsf.gov)

The National Science Foundation "promotes the progress of science; to advance the national health, prosperity, and welfare; to secure the national defense . . ." The foundation continually keeps scientific discovery at an edge.

Contact Information:
National Science Foundation
4201 Wilson Blvd
Arlington, VA 22230
Tel: (703) 292-5111, (800) 877-8339
info@nsf.gov

Links for parents and teachers:

http://www.nsf.gov/news/classroom/

This site provides materials in every interest-area for lesson plans and at-home activities.

National Science Teacher's Association (www.nsta.org)

The National Science Teacher's Association promotes excellence in science teaching. The website provides information about how to strengthen the quality of science and teaching.

Contact Information:
NSTA
1840 Wilson Boulevard
Arlington, VA 22201-3000
Tel: (703) 243.7100

Links for parents and teachers:

http://www.nsta.org/classroomdoors

This link provides additional websites related to teaching science and is tailored to a specific area and grade level.

Science Service (www.sciserv.org)

The mission of Science Service is to advance the understanding and appreciation of science. In addition to its education programs, Science Service maintains a listing of science training programs for students and teachers. This non-profit also publishes the weekly magazine *Science News* and the online publication *Science News for Kids*.

Contact Information:
Science Service
1719 N Street, NW
Washington, DC 20036
Tel: (202) 785-2255

United States Geological Survey (http://www.usgs.gov/)

The USGS attempts to provide accurate and useful information about the Earth. They use this information to help reduce damage from natural disasters and to manage natural resources.

Contact Information:
To email questions, use the form at http://www.usgs.gov/ask/index.html.
Tel: (888) 275-8747

Museums and Shows

The Association of Science-Technology Centers (http://www.astc.org)
The ASTC is an organization devoted to furthering the awareness of science to as diverse an audience as possible. Using this site, parents and teachers can find hands-on science centers near them.

Exploratorium.edu
This site is an online extension of the Exploratorium science museum. The site makes it possible for the museum's demonstrations of phenomena, experiments, and scientific information to reach both homes and schools.

Contact Information:
The Exploratorium
3601 Lyon Street
San Francisco, CA 94123
Tel: (415) 563-7337

Links for parents and teachers:
http://www.exploratorium.edu/educate/index.html

FOSS (Full Option Science System) http://www.lawrencehallofscience.org/foss/
FOSS is a research-based science program for grades K–8 developed at the Lawrence Hall of Science, University of California at Berkeley. FOSS is also an ongoing research project dedicated to improving the learning and teaching of science.

Contact Information:
Lawrence Hall of Science
University of California
Berkeley, CA 94720
Tel: (510) 642-8941
Fax: (510) 642-7387

Museum of Science, Boston (http://www.mos.org/)
The Museum of Science in Boston offers many virtual exhibits. Within each exhibit children, parents, and teachers can explore with activities, general information, and special links for further resources on a particular subject.

Contact Information:
Museum of Science
Science Park
Boston, MA 02114
Tel: (617) 723-2500
information@mos.org

Links for parents and teachers:

http://www.mos.org/?audience=educators
This link provides a variety of educator tools such as an educator resource center and field trip guides to the museum.

Physics Van (http://van.hep.uiuc.edu/)

The Physics Van is a traveling physics show for children. The show demonstrates how physics pertains to everyday life and to explain why the world works the way it does. On this website, there is also an online show children and adults can view.

Contact Information:

PhysVan@uiuc.edu This email address will reach all members of the Physics Van.
jakubas@uiuc.edu
Tel: (217) 333-1104
for scheduling shows, general info, web issues, online services, demos, equipment and research.

Links for parents and teachers:

http://van.hep.uiuc.edu/
This link provides a list of websites for teachers who want to find additional resources, activities, and information about physics including physics videos, physics toys for demonstrations, games, and puzzles!

Science Websites

TryScience.org

TryScience.org offers online interactivity with science and technology centers around the world. The site allows children to discover and experiment with science while providing a great science education.

Links for parents and teachers:

http://www.tryscience.org/parents/parent.html
This link guides parents on how to give their children a great science education.
http://www.tryscience.org/teachers/teacher.html
This link explains how to use TryScience in a classroom.

Weatherworks.com

Weatherworks.com is a site dedicated to educational weather services for teachers and students from pre-schoolers to adults.

Contact Information:
H. Mike Mogil
How the Weatherworks
2979 Mona Lisa Boulevard
Naples, FL 34119
Tel: (239) 592-6636, (301) 637-4523

Links for parents and teachers:

http://www.weatherworks.com/services/services_overview.html

Wonderquest.com

Wonderquest.com features a weekly science column on usatoday.com. The website also contains an index of science questions, a glossary of scientific terms, and a list of top-ten science questions.

Contact Information:
April Holladay
c/o UPS Store
3301-R Coors Rd. NW
Albuquerque, NM 87120
Tel: (505) 831-2640 (MST)
Fax: (928) 223 -0160
contact@wonderquest.com

Science Equipment and Supplies

Educational Innovations

(http://www.teachersource.com)

Founded in 1994, this catalog, available both online and through the mail, features over 1,000 educational science products and books, with new products being constantly added.

Frey Scientific Elementary

(http://www.freyscientific.com)

In Frey Scientific Elementary, teachers will find an exceptional array of products aimed at students in grades 3-6. Especially interesting are their new Performance Series kits, in areas such as Life and Earth Science.

Nasco Science

(http://www.enasco.com)

The Nasco Science catalog is only one of the company's many diverse education-oriented catalogs. It features an enormous selection of science tools for the classroom as well as extremely budget-oriented pricing. To request a catalog, call 1-800-558-9595.

Schoolmasters Science

(http://www.schoolmasters.com)

This diverse catalog features lab supplies, experiment kits, microscopes, anatomy models and other high-quality science products. To order a catalog, call 1-800-521-2832.

Science Kit

(http://www.sciencekit.com)

In this huge catalog, educators can browse a high-quality selection of science tools and books for grades K-6. The catalog itself features activities and hundreds of "teaching tips." To request a catalog, send an email to sk@sciencekit.com.

Index

A

AAAS (American Association for the Advancement of Science), 139
acid, mixing with base, 76
acid, measuring of, 65–66
adenosine triphosphate (ATP), 45
air density, 81–82
alkaline, measuring of, 65–66
Allen, Paul, 128
altitude, in determining location, 107
American Association for the Advancement of Science (AAAS), 139
amphibians, 39
AMU (atomic mass unit), 73
Anaximander, 130
angle of incidence, 134
angle of reflection, 134
Animalia, 36
Antarctica, 109–110, 112
antibiotics, 55
anti-inflammatory components, in breastmilk, 41
arachnids, 39
Archimedes, 95
Archimedes's principle, 95–96
arteries, 50–51
Association of Science-Technology Centers, The (ASTC), 144
ASTC (Association of Science-Technology Centers, The), 144
atmosphere, 104–105
atomic mass, 73
atomic mass unit (AMU), 73
atomic number, 67
atoms, and radioactive decay, 73–74
ATP (adenosine triphosphate), 45
atria, 51
auricle, 51
axis, Earth, 101

B

bacteria, 54
Balaenoptera musculus. see blue whale
Banneker, Benjamin, 38
base (alkaline), 66
mixing with acid, 76

bats, 44
batteries, creation of, 92
Beethoven, Ludwig van, 97–98
Bell, Alexander Graham, 129
birds, 39
blood, 49, 50–51
blue whale, 43
bodily fluids, 49
bones, importance of calcium in, 65
breastmilk, 41–42
bridges, arch-shaped, 94–95

C

calcium, 65
calcium oxalate, 68
calendars, religious, 101–102
calories, 66
carbon, 68, 72, 89
carbon 14, 73–74
carbon cycle, 45–46
carbon dating, 73–74
carbon dioxide, 45, 51, 74
carbon monoxide, 74
Carnegie Academy for the Advancement of Science (CASE), 139–140
carnivore, 132
CASE (Carnegie Academy for the Advancement of Science), 139–140
cast iron, 71
CAT scans (computerized axial tomography) 86
CDC (Centers for Disease Control), 140
celestial motion, 100–101
Celsius, 123
body temperature, 51
boiling point of water, 60
Centers for Disease Control (CDC), 140
Centrigade scale, 123
centripetal force, 84
cephalothorax, 39
chemical change, examples of, 76–77
Chinese, discovery of cast iron, 71
Christian calendar, 101–102
circulatory system, 50–51
circumference, 108–109
Clarke, Sir Arthur C., 111
classes, 36

O

P

R

S

About the Authors

Dia Michels is the founder and president of Platypus Media, an independent press in Washington, DC, whose goal is to create and distribute materials that promote family life by educating grown-ups about infant development and by teaching children about the world around them. She is an award-winning science writer who has written or edited over a dozen books for adults and children. Her titles include *Breastfeeding at a Glance: Facts, Figures and Trivia about Breastfeeding, Milk, Money and Madness: The Culture and Politics of Breastfeeding,* and *If My Mom Were a Platypus: Mammal Babies and Their Mothers.* She teaches family science classes at children's and science museums around the US. She has spoken at national and international conferences for such groups as American Association for the Advancement of Science, National Association of Biology Teachers, La Leche League International, Smithsonian Institution, and the Museum of Science. Dia lives in Washington, DC, with her husband and their three children. She can be reached at **Dia@PlatypusMedia.com.**

Nathan Levy is the author of *Stories with Holes, Whose Clues?* and *Nathan Levy's 100 Intriguing Questions.* A gifted educator, Nathan worked directly with children, teachers and parents in his thirty five years as a teacher and principal. He has developed unique teaching strategies that encouraged the love of learning. He has also mentored more than thirty current principals and superintendents, as well as helped to train thousands of teachers and parents in better ways to help children learn. For the past thirty years, Nathan has led workshops at state and national education conferences all over the world. When hired to conduct school-based and district service, his ideas have helped raise pupil achievement and restore enthusiasm to the educational staff. Nathan has done workshops in the areas of reading language arts, social studies, math, critical thinking, gifted, special education, classroom management and is available for parent and business conferences. He can be reached at **Nathan@PlatypusMedia.com.**

Editorial Staff

Senior Editor:	Becca Tarsa, Washington, DC
Associate Editor:	Alexandra Simpson, Washington, DC
Project Management:	Gretchen Hesbacher, Washington, DC
Cover, Book Design and Illustration:	Andrew Barthelmes, Peekskill, NY
Lead Researcher:	Janelle Hatton, Montclair, VA
Associate Researchers:	KC Johnson, Arlington, VA
	Janell Robisch, Luray, VA
	Kathy Savage, Mechanicsburg, PA
	Leslie Teitel, Alexandria, VA
Student Readers:	Arianna Efstathiou, Age 14, Ogunquit, ME
	Sophie Ord, Age 16, Oakville, Ontario, Canada
	Josh Samors, Age 15, Silver Spring, MD
	Alex Spanjer, Age 12, Dalton, GA
	Ben Spector, Age 15, Ithaca, NY
	Lena Sessions, Age 17, Eugene, OR

About Science, Naturally!™

Science, Naturally!™ is committed to increasing science literacy by exploring and demystifying key science topics. Our mission is to produce products—for children and adults alike—that are filled with interesting facts, important insights and key connections in science. Our materials are designed to make potentially intimidating topics intriguing and accessible. Our products are perfect for kids, parents, educators, and anyone interested in gaining a better understanding of how science affects everyday life.

Our first title, *If My Mom Were a Platypus: Mammal Babies and their Mothers*, won an "NSTA Recommends" award by the National Science Teachers' Association and has been featured by the American Association for the Advancement of Science, the Carnegie Academy for Science Education, as well as in science, children's and natural history museums around the country.

Our next title in the series is *101 Things Everyone Should Know About Math*, which will help readers of all ages enjoy and understand basic mathematical operations. Using a simple question and answer format, *101 Things Everyone Should Know About Math* is a great tool that makes understanding math easy and fun. Watch for upcoming titles in the series on history, world events, and culture.

For more information about our publications, contact us for a catalog or visit us at www.ScienceNaturally.com.

Teaching the science of everyday life

Science, Naturally!
627 A Street, NE
Washington, DC 20002
202-465-4798
Toll-free: 1-866-SCI-9876
(1-866-724-9876)
Fax: 202-558-2132
Info@ScienceNaturally.com
www.ScienceNaturally.com

We are always looking for engaging questions for our "101 Things Everyone Should Know" series. Submit a question for our math, social studies, language arts titles, or for *101 **More** Things Everyone Should Know About Science*. If we use it, we'll send you a free copy of the book in which it appears.

Email your question to:

> 101Things@ScienceNaturally.com

Or send it to us at:

> 101 Things Submission
> Science, Naturally!
> 627 A Street, NE
> Washington, DC 20002
> 202- 465-4798
> Toll-free: 1-866-SCI-9876 (1-866-724-9876)
> Fax: 202-558-2132
> Info@ScienceNaturally.com
> www.ScienceNaturally.com

Test Booklet Information

Use *101 Things Everyone Should Know About Science* with a group of students!

Science, Naturally!™ has created a student test booklet, available for classroom, home-school, after-school, or science club use.

The 16-page booklet includes all 106 questions from this book. Use as a single write-in test booklet or have students write the answers on a separate sheet.

Order today!

QUANTITY	PRICE
1	$2.95
2–9	$2.50
10–49	$2.25
50–99	$2.00
100–249	$1.75
250–499	$1.50
500–999	$1.00
1000+	Contact Us

Bulk Purchase Info

Schools, libraries, government and non-profit organizations may receive a bulk discount for quantity orders. Please contact us at Info@ScienceNaturally.com.

COMING SOON from Science, Naturally!™

101 Things Everyone Should Know About Math
By Barbara G. Levine, H. Michael Mogil and Nathan Levy

Change for a twenty, thirty minutes on a parking meter, six apples for
three dollars or a 'bakers dozen' for six dollars... Math is a critical part of
our everyday lives; we use it dozens of times a day—and wish we
understood it better. The second in the "101 Things Everyone Should
Know" series, this book helps readers of all ages enjoy and understand
basic mathematical operations. Using a simple question and answer
format, *101 Things Everyone Should Know About Math* is a great tool that
makes understanding math easy and fun. It is perfect for kids, parents,
grown-ups, students, teachers, and anyone interested in the difference
between an Olympic event score of 9.0 and a Richter scale score of 9.0.

Barbara G. Levine is an award-
winning math educator.

H. Michael Mogil is a
meteorologist and experienced
math tutor.

Nathan Levy is a seasoned
educator and author of
numerous books in education.

Ages 8-108. Paperback, 160 pages.
ISBN-10: 0-9678020-3-2
ISBN-13: 978-0-9678020-3-9
$9.95
Second in the series which
includes these topics: science,
history, world events,
and culture.